From Stand-Up Comedian to Stand-Up Teacher

BY: MIKE RIVERA

With: Craig Sidorowicz

Published by Richter Publishing LLC www.richterpublishing.com

Editors: Mandi Weems & Monica San Nicolas

Formatted by: Diana Fisler & Monica San Nicolas

Copyright © 2015 Mike Rivera & Craig Sidorowicz

ISBN: 0692610863
ISBN-13: 9780692610862

DISCLAIMER

This book is designed to provide information on teaching and comedy only. This information is provided and sold with the knowledge that the publisher and author do not offer any legal or medical advice. In the case of a need for any such expertise, consult with the appropriate professional. This book does not contain all information available on the subject. This book has not been created to be specific to any individual's or organization's situation or needs. Every effort has been made to make this book as accurate as possible. However, there may be typographical and or content errors. Therefore, this book should serve only as a general guide and not as the ultimate source of subject information. This book contains information that might be dated and is intended only to educate and entertain. The author and publisher shall have no liability or responsibility to any person or entity regarding any loss or damage incurred, or alleged to have incurred, directly or indirectly, by the information contained in this book. You hereby agree to be bound by this disclaimer or you may return this book within the guarantee time period for a full refund. Some characters appearing in this work are fictitious. Any resemblance to real persons, living or dead, is purely coincidental. Photos of any and all person appearing in this work has acquired permission from such persons or was previously published in a public forum.

DEDICATION

To my children, Brendon and Caitlin, who have brought the words "unconditional love" to life for me.

~

To all of the teachers and comedians who go above and beyond every day. You are noticed and appreciated.

CONTENTS

ACKNOWLEDGMENTS

All my life, I've heard people say: "I'm going to write a book one day." They never do. Why? Because it's hard. It's that plain and simple. You have a blank screen, and you have to fill it. What a challenge! There are days you want to give up. So many other things come up that have to be put on the back burner. Writing this book has been a case study in perseverance for me. I could not have done it alone.

I would like to thank my friend, Fred Reiss, who has given the fight of his life in battling cancer. He is wonderful author, comic, and friend. Through his books and comedy, he advocates the enduring spirit of "never giving up." He is a true inspiration.

I would like to thank Les McCurdy and Susan Hentz. They gave me the confidence and support to write the book from the academic and comedic side. They basically got in my face and said: "You are a great comic and a great teacher. You are America's Most Hilarious Teacher! So, write a book."

I would like to thank Tara Richter. Bumping into her was no coincidence. I was starting to a write book and she just happened to be a publisher. She would always send me notes of encouragement throughout this whole process.

I would like to thank fellow comedian/teacher, Bill Kilpatrick, for his invaluable insights and contributions with the STAND-UP strategies.

I would especially like to thank my good friend and fellow teacher, Craig Sidorowicz, aka: "Mr. Sid." He is an incredible teacher. He is able to blend the academic and social aspects of instruction. I purposely chose him to teach my son and my daughter. He was their rock in the 6th grade during their transition from elementary school to middle school. I also intentionally chose him to help me write this book. The book would only be half of what it is without him. He is disciplined and never cuts corners. He is one of the few people I trust with his critiques.

That is a friend. I cannot thank him enough.

Finally, to all my friends and family who I could always count on their support along this wonderful journey. Also, like Beethoven, I would like to thank my "Immortal Beloved" who has opened up my eyes to see and enjoy the little things in life. You are my home.

FOREWORD

Mike Rivera is a funny man. He has made me laugh until my sides hurt and tears have rolled down my cheeks. He is also an exceptional educator. Mike and I have been friends for over 35 years and I have watched his journey of perseverance in achieving excellence in teaching while celebrating his love for humor. This book captures how Mike was able to use his sharp wit, quirky and versatile background as an educator and Dad, to help students succeed. His success inside and out of the classroom has helped other educators create environments where learning is fun.

Mike's STAND-UP technique is a breakthrough to students and teachers, reinvigorating the classroom with optimism, laughter, and most importantly, a solid educational foundation for their future. This book shares his ideas of how you can bring your "funny" out in the classroom.

Reaching students in our tech-driven society poses new challenges. Teachers have to compete with a global offering of endless *YouTube* clips. They are feeling less supported and their creativity has been dampened by the overwhelming testing culture. Mike reminds us that human connection, humor, empathy, and never taking oneself too seriously, is always the key to student success. Classrooms are magical places where teachers and students learn from one another. Mike recognizes that and uses humor to make that learning experience one that drives students to be lifelong learners achieving their own brand of success.

Mike uses these techniques at a pivotal time, middle school. Students have many different influences during those adolescents' years, but a teacher is someone with whom a student spends most of their day. Mike understands that humor and the positive impact his techniques bring to the classroom help students stay on course and focus on learning. Although his experience is in the middle school grades, his approach can be utilized in any learning modality.

Mikes shares his antidotes about his journey to become a comedian and how he was influenced by greats like Robin Williams, and Bob Saget from *Full House*. In this book, Mike explains how those early years of comedic training influenced his teaching and how important that was to bringing humor into the classroom. He also reminds us that many of his own teachers, perhaps not well known or celebrated, guided him with Yoda-esque directives, like "Go see the world and come back to teach..." Mike has the benefit of merging his two passions to create a successful career in both fields, and now wants to help his fellow teachers find their own beat in the classroom.

When you read this book, you will discover your own funny bone and help students succeed while enjoying the process. With an open mind and heart, channel your own humor into the classroom and never forget teaching and learning should be fun.

Lars A. Hafner, Ph.D.
- Former Legislator, Florida State House of Representatives
- Former College President, State College of Florida
- Political Analyst, CBS Affiliate, WTSP, Channel 10
- Tampa / St. Petersburg, FL

PREFACE

From Stand-up Comic to Stand-up Teacher is the story of Mike Rivera, "America's Most Hilarious Teacher." Talented and experienced in the worlds of both comedy and teaching, Mike brings together the unique perspectives of a nationally touring stand-up comedian, and an award-winning teacher, with the purpose of invigorating today's American classroom. He calls this "The Comedy/Teaching Craft" and "The STAND-UP Strategies."

In Part 1 of this book, I will tell you the story of my comedic roots, and how destiny led me on the path to teaching. Growing up, I had two passions in life, the love of history and the love of stand-up comedy. From my early youth, I was always reading anything that had to do with history, especially stories of the American Revolution and the Civil War. My father would take me around the country to visit many historical battlefields and museums. Anytime there would be a new television show or movie about history, I had to see it. In school, my teachers reinforced my love of history by mentoring and giving me assignments that were challenging and engaging. During my senior year in high school, my favorite social studies teacher, Larry Williams, instilled me with the idea of one day coming back to teach.

I developed my appreciation of stand-up comedy by listening to Bill Cosby records as far back as the first grade. Once again, my father played an important part in my love for comedy. We would always watch the latest stand-up comics on network television together. With the advent of cable television, I was able to fully appreciate the talents of stand-up comedians through their hour-long specials on HBO. Being able to see the uncensored full performances of great comedians like Steve Martin, and my idol, Robin Williams, fueled my ambition to one day get on stage.

It was in college, while attending San Jose State University, that I was able to see and appreciate the intricacies and craftsmanship of stand-up comedians. The *Last Laugh* comedy club was only a mile from campus. I went to shows every Sunday night to watch and learn. I found that the comedians were always approachable and gave advice on how to get into the business.

After getting my degree in communications, I knew I wanted to be a comedian. The San Francisco/Bay Area comedy scene was one of the top breeding grounds for performers in the country. I had to hone my craft by going to amateur nights for two years before eventually getting a break and becoming the House MC at the Last Laugh. Here, I would have the advantage of performing in front of a packed room of over 200 people a night. Through the Last Laugh, I was able to develop a network of friends, contacts, and connections that would help me break into the industry. For the next eight years, I would tour the United States, the Caribbean, and Europe as a professional stand-up comedian.

Through comedy, I met my first wife. I knew that for this marriage to be successful, I would have to come off the road and settle down. But what would I do? It was a no-brainer for me. I remembered the advice of my favorite teacher, Larry Williams, to see the world and come back and teach. I went back to school and got my teaching certification in grades 6-12 social studies.

In Part 2 of my book, I will discuss the evolution and the techniques that led me to the remarkable breakthrough of the Comedy/Teaching Craft and the STAND-UP Strategies. Like any other teacher, it took me a couple of years to learn the basics. During my first year of teaching middle school social studies, I noticed that many of the same strategies I honed as a stand-up comic could be useful in the classroom. Over the years, I discovered that using these techniques and strategies had a positive effect on my classroom dynamics.

I further developed The Comedy/Teaching Craft into a collection of seven concise dimensions called: The STAND-UP Strategies. Using the strategies, I was able to see real gains in the areas of classroom discipline, engagement, and higher student achievement. There were other benefits outside of the classroom: I wasn't as tired at the end of the day as I used to be. I also learned to collaborate positively with my fellow colleagues, to maintain focus, and to avoid slipping into the doldrums of "educational burnout."

In the third part of this book, I will unveil and discuss each of The STAND-UP Strategies. For each strategy, I will demonstrate The Comedy/Teaching Craft to its fullest extent. Each strategy chapter will begin with a common classroom problem. I'll then relate it to my experiences from the world of stand-up comedy and discuss how I was able to solve the problem. I'll then bring it back to the classroom to give practical, realistic examples on how to use The Comedy/Teaching Craft to solve the classroom problem. Each strategy will have a review and section and dedicated reflection questions to help teachers further develop and enhance their teaching.

In the 4th and final part of the book, I will go beyond my strategies to discuss real life issues and inspirations in my life. You, the reader, will gain insight into dealing with what many comics and teachers believe to be an obstacle with profession: the heckler. I'll show you how the simple act of taking a moment to have fun can have a lasting impact on a child. Then, I will impart the tried and true wisdom of my father's virtues, and discuss how I share his legacy with my children and students.

You will learn the story of how a simple middle school teacher, who also happens to perform stand-up comedy, can wind up on network television to become "America's Most Hilarious Teacher." Finally, in a poignant yet simple essay, I will tell you why, even with offers to perform comedy around the country, I still prefer to teach.

INTRODUCTION
BLINDSIDED

"Are you going to leave us?"

Those were the first words I heard from my students the Monday I returned from New York. After being on national television for week, and winning the "America's Most Hilarious Teacher" contest on ABC's *The View*, I was expecting cheers and high-fives. They'd just seen me on television performing stand-up, winning the competition, and finally having my own sit-down segment with Joy Behar in the show's comedy spotlight. The whole school cheered when they announced me as the winner. I had local television camera crews meeting me at the airport. I had three camera crews in my classroom doing background segments on me for the evening news. The students were all excited before I left for New York... So, what happened?

I was so looking forward to coming back to school after a whirlwind week on *The View*. So, with head high and chest puffed out, I was ready for a great day at school. The bell rang for class. The students were strangely quiet. I was sitting on a stool in front of the class, which was a cue to the students that I was comfortable answering any questions about my new adventures.

Right away, I noticed a certain disconnect with them. I was perplexed. I had spent six months developing a great classroom dynamic of openness. So, I just asked: "Does anyone have any questions?" There was silence, and after 30 seconds (or what seemed like an hour to me), a student in the back raised his hand and asked: "Are you going to leave us?"

After a few seconds, another student in the front asked: "Yeah, you leaving us?" It took me a minute, but then I got it. This was my Sidney Poitier moment from *To Sir with Love*, when Mr. Thackeray tells the students he's accepted another job after he'd been the one constant and role model in his students' lives. I'm not saying I was Mr. Thackeray, but I could identify. They weren't upset about potentially losing their teacher. They were upset by the potential of losing what I had brought to them as an adult who cared about them, who advocated for them, who accepted them for who they were: a teacher who could make them laugh and learn at the same time.

"No, I won't leave you," I told them. I proceeded to discuss the opportunities I'd now been given and all of them required me to move. With two kids, ages nine and 11, I knew I could not be a good father if was on the road as a nationally-touring headlining comedian. That would not be an option. I would stay with my kids at home, and with my kids at school.

I always knew I'd had good relationships with my students, but it wasn't until that moment that I realized that true impact I had on them as a teacher. I was overwhelmed by the feeling of great responsibility that teachers have. The importance we play in the lives of our students is something that standardized tests can never measure. It is the reason many of us still teach.

PART I
My Comedic Roots

CHAPTER 1

COMEDY

Beginnings and Early Influences:

I have always loved comedy, and my family members have always been big fans. My cousins enjoyed Bill Cosby, and we would listen to his albums as early as the 1st grade. I was hooked. Whenever there was a stand-up on a variety show, we would always watch. Another one of my early favorites was Don Rickles. He was fast-paced, and would take no prisoners on stage. His act was not very politically correct, and wouldn't make it in today's world, but back then, it was funny. I loved Flip Wilson and his ability to incorporate characters into his routine.

I was never a big fan of the "Borscht Belt" comedy scene. Those are the ones you would see playing on the Poconos, the resorts that the "East Coast people" would vacation to, which would show up on Ed Sullivan and make my dad just stare. They had material, but they weren't funny people. Now, seeing Phyllis Diller, that was funny! It was her character and her blend of material that I found myself drawn to.

My father was always a big fan of the Smothers Brothers. They were clean-cut, but their material was edgy and political. Their show would showcase a wide array of artists that were not mainstream. I loved David Fry. He was an incredible impressionist who added a political twist to his material. He was funny and smart. My family and I loved Pat Paulsen. His deadpan, *Droopy-Dog*, self-deprecating humor was just so funny. I couldn't wait for the times when he would drop in on a sketch comedy bit for the show. He would always steal the scene. Many years later, I had the opportunity of working with Pat. He was wonderful. When I would bring up certain sketches from the Smothers Brothers that I'd watched when I was seven, his eyes would just open up and he'd smile. He spoke at length on how the sketches were written and developed. It showed me the keen awareness it took to be funny. To this day, I still treasure his comedic ability, his kindness, and his insights.

Robin on the Mount:

One of my biggest influences in my life came from an experience I had while I was attending San Jose State University in California. I was listening to the radio one day, and they mentioned that Robin Williams would be doing a benefit in Marin County, about 60 miles away. Robin was my favorite comic. I loved Mork & Mindy. I loved how at any time, he could just go off and do the unexpected and make it funny. When it came to being quick-witted, Robin was second to none. If I thought I was funny, then Robin was my Yoda. I made it to the show with a friend from my dorm, and we were able to move up to the front of the theatre since the event was a last minute decision. There were only about 200 people there, and the room was only about half full. When Robin hit the stage it was magical. He was fast, quick, and never mean on stage. How many comics can say that? He would have the audience ask him questions, take five minutes to answer them, and go off into his own comical genius world. I watched intently and was completely floored by Robin. He made it seem so effortless, as if he just got up and did an hour off the top of his head. I was hooked. Somehow, someway, I wanted to get into stand-up and be like Robin. There was one big problem: I was scared to death of being in front of people and riddled with anxiety.

Taking the Leap of Faith:

So, how did I become a comic? My father was a great supporter. He always taught me to turn my greatest weakness into my greatest strength. It also helped that a mile away from the college was a full time comedy club called the *Last Laff*. I would spend my senior year going every Sunday night. I was exposed to all types and styles of comedy. I was also fortunate to live in the San Francisco Bay Area, which had an incredible comedy scene, and was located within two hours of about twenty different full time and weekend comedy clubs.

One evening after a watching a show, I saw a flyer about an improvisation workshop that was starting up. It was run by local Radio DJ Dan Schow. I felt that being on stage with an improvisation group would provide strength in numbers, as opposed to going up all by myself, which terrified me. So, I spent over a year and a half going to improv class twice a week. I thought it was bit hokey and not as funny as what I wanted. That's how I realized that not all improv people were like Robin Williams. There will only be one Robin Williams.

Eventually, I knew it was time for me to go solo and hit the stage. For someone who suffers from anxiety issues, this would be a tremendous step. I had my friend David Fusilier, a gifted writer to this day, help me with my material and organize the flow of it. I had to come up with five minutes of material and find open mics (amateur comedy nights) where I could find stage time. Finding venues to perform was not the problem, but gathering the courage to perform on stage was. It took me six months from the time that I said I'd go up on stage until the time I actually did it. I would look for every excuse to delay my introduction to stand-up comedy.

I found a local place in San Jose, CA. There weren't that many people there. I had all the support of my comic friends, who were like family. They were all starting out, too. It was like being in high school, and we were freshman once again. I was so nervous I wanted to vomit, which I would do for the first two years of performing at open mics. To my surprise, my first show went fine. I learned, like everything, that improvement will take time. The key was to get that first laugh, and it would calm me down. It was amazing. The power to make an audience laugh was so addicting to me. It made me feel special. On stage, I was an exaggeration of the extrovert that was always hiding in me. Once I was hooked, I went all in. I would drive many hours to get as much stage time as possible. This is what it would take if I ever wanted to become a professional standup comedian.

My first real break came when I was asked to be one of the rotating hosts at the *Last Laff* in San Jose. It was my home club. I would get to perform 6 nights a week in front of crowds of over 200 people. I got to work with the top club and TV comics from around the country. The first comic I worked with was Bob Saget of *Full House* fame. He could not have been nicer. It was such a great experience because I had to warm up the audience from scratch. That does take skill. I had to draw them in and capture their attention. Since I didn't have a lot of time, I had to develop a fast style of comedy, so my key was to get so many laughs as I could per minute. My goal was to start from five minutes, then get to twenty to be an opening act, thirty to be a feature act, and finally to 45 to be a headliner. I was very lucky to get my feet wet in such a professional club as the *Last Laff*. It was my home club that gave me my first chance, and I will never forget it.

After a year and a half, I moved to the San Francisco Bay Area to be closer to that incredible comedy scene. It was ultra-competitive. Certain clubs would have their favorite comics, which I thought was a bit insane, but that's how the world works. I learned that it wasn't the funniest people that got the breaks, but the ones who were willing to cozy up to the promoters. I was really never good at that starting out. I believed if you were funny, then you were funny, and that is the end of that. I was young and naïve: The comics who can be funny and network are the ones who got the auditions and breaks.

Holy City Zoo:

My hang out for my time in San Francisco was the *Holy City Zoo*. It was a hole in the wall, which could fit about 40 people at most. But it's where Robin Williams would go to practice, and he considered it his home club. That was enough for me. It became my Mecca. For the next two and a half years, I worked on writing, writing, and writing. I loved current events and wanted to be a staff writer on *any* nighttime show. I would come to the Zoo with my notebook and get to try new material three to four times a week. The other nights, I would be either getting opening work, or going to open mics to work on my set.

I had always heard the Robin Williams would come down every once in a while. I was too wrapped up in trying to get my stand-up career off the ground, so it had become just a passing thought. One night when I arrived at the *Holy City Zoo*, a couple of the other young comics said that Robin was next door looking at some books. About 20 minutes later, while about five of us were hanging out in front of the club, Robin came by. All the comics nodded their heads and tried their best to keep that cool distance. This was extremely difficult because every ounce of me just wanted to say: "Oh my God...I'm making small talk with Robin Williams." But that was the way he wanted it. You could tell when he was in his private mode that he just wanted to be like any other comic. So, he asked if he could do some time in front of the 20 people in the audience (of course he could!). The host announced his name, and the 20 sounded like 200.

What was so great about it was that Robin treated the small audience like it was an HBO special. He only knew one speed to go. From the side of the stage, only 10 feet away, I stood and marveled. Throughout the next two years, he would frequent the clubs every couple of months, and was always humble, if not a tad shy. In return, the comics would give him his space and freedom to relax from being the superstar that he was. When he would come down and give you the nod of familiarity, it was like being blessed from the Pope.

One of my favorite stories happened when my sister and her husband were visiting from Florida. I told them I would be at the *Zoo* till about midnight. There were about five comics hanging out that night. Robin showed up with Dennis Miller. Dennis was white hot doing the news on *Saturday Night Live* back then. I remember sitting on the bench, and by now I knew the *Zoo* drill. As a comic you never act "in awe" of anyone. You just treat them like any other comic. I was sitting on the bench looking over notes and Dennis asked if he could sit down. I said: "Sure," and after a couple of minutes we were making small talk about the writing for *Weekend Update*.

So, about this time, I saw my sister and her husband coming up the street. I got up to greet them, and their eyes were wide with shock. I told Robin and Dennis that this was my sister and her husband from Florida. They were kind of enough to shake hands with my family and exchange pleasantries for a couple of minutes. I remember that night I got a call at five in the morning from my mother in Florida. She relayed that my sister had called her and said: "Mom, you'll never believe who Michael hangs out with!" We were just at the right place at the right time.

In the pecking order of *Holy City Zoo* comics I was obviously very low, but I prided myself on hanging out with, and being a part of the *Zoo* family. Some of the best comics I have ever seen came from the *Zoo*. Some made it big, and others did not. They were funny and had a great influence over me. To this day, Larry "Bubbles" Brown is one of the funniest men this Earth has ever produced. His quaint, defeatist, bitter attitude drew quite a following of minion comics. I proud to say I was one of them.

A Shot:

Because of my penchant for writing current events, one of my friends recommended that I audition for the *Late Show* as a writer. They told me to read the morning papers and submit my material by noon. I got a call around 5:00 pm. The producer started talking salary and bonuses. I was on cloud nine. I told my roommates not to say a word, as I very superstitious. They did. The following Monday, I got a call from the producer. He informed me that they were going with a more experienced writer. As a young comic, this crushed me. I should have moved to Los Angeles right away and keep pursuing my writing, but instead I decided to get down on myself and get away. It is one of the few regrets I have in my life. I use this story with my students as an example of how to learn to overcome obstacles and persevere.

Instead of going to L.A. and pursuing an "industry job," I started to get club bookings in the Bay Area and around the West Coast. Within two years, I was a fulltime road comic, featuring at clubs all around the country, the Caribbean, and even Europe. I had incredible experiences and many wonderful stories... but that's for another book. I ended up meeting my wife at a club in the Cayman Islands in the early nineties. When I decided to get married, I knew that being on the road for 40 weeks per year was not the way to start a marriage. So, what would I do?

*Mike Rivera on "Daytime"

*Mike Rivera with Rob Schneider

*Mike Rivera with Jay Pharoah from "Saturday Night Live"

*Mike Rivera with Tom Cotter, Finalist from "America's Got Talent"

*Mike Rivera backstage Pre-Show

*Headlining at the IMPROV

CHAPTER 2
SEE THE WORLD AND COME BACK AND TEACH

"See the world and come back and teach!" Those were the words of my favorite teacher, Larry Williams. He taught 11th grade American History. I appreciated him because he accepted me for who I was, and always encouraged me to follow my path. It meant a lot for a teacher to say: "it's okay to be outside the box." Did I drive him crazy? Sure, but it was okay. He was showing me how to open doors in life. As a teacher, I have tried to keep Larry's mission alive. Just as in *Ghostbusters*, we teachers are the key masters.

A quick wit and the ability to think on my feet were skills that I started developing in the early days of my childhood. It was this type of humor that got me through high school, college, touring nationally as a headliner, and eventually helped me develop my own style of teaching.

I was not the class clown during my years growing up in public school. Instead, I would be the one who would cut up the class clown, and verbally tear him to shreds to my close friends. That was the difference between class clown and myself, the class clown would be laughed at, and while I would get the laughs for the funny things I would say. I was like a comedic assassin. To most people, I was quiet, shy, and under the radar, but to my friends I was the one who would be the first to whisper something funny as soon as it happened.

In the classroom, I was always observant of other people. I liked to see what made them tick. I guess I was starting my comedy observations at an early age. I was never one to seek massive attention. Like most kids, I was trying to see where I fit in. I had a small circle of friends and found myself relating more to the teachers. Looking back, I believe it was because my sense of humor was mature and I enjoyed being around smart people. The teachers always showed me respect and were real with me. I could always count on a well-thought-out answer anytime I would ask them a question. This is something I kept with me when I became a teacher.

The Talent Show:

It was in my junior year of high school where I really started to find my niche. I had neighborhood friends who were also in my class that enjoyed the same style of music. This time period was the early stages of Punk Rock Era. It was different. It wasn't mainstream. I could relate. So, we all started to take guitar lessons and began playing together. Every year our school had a talent show. My friends and I thought: *What a great way to leave our mark on John Jay High School!* Our premise was: "What could we do that would totally offend everyone and just that blow the audience away?"

Our band's name was Shet. Yes, go with the double entendre. Our song was called "Funk You!" and we would interchange the "n" with the "c" as soon as we hit the stage. We had KISS-influenced pyrotechnics. Our performance would have six flash bombs, a band member that would blow a fireball like Gene Simmons of KISS does, a strobe light in a 6'x4' fixture that would flash our band's name. We never worked so hard in our lives to get something done. We auditioned with a different song to get us on the bill. Our master plan was in place.

The night of the show, we had six band members. Only four were playing real instruments. We had three friends who would help us set up the stage, and a pyrotechnic kid who would electronically set off the flash bombs.

I was excited the night of the show, but would soon be short lived. When I arrived and met up with our group it wasn't hard to tell that half of them were either drunk or high. This was commonplace for the *Dazed and Confused* time period. We were the first act after the intermission. We had 10 minutes to set up. We started our performance, and right away, the flash bombs were not going off. I was playing guitar. My friend Rick was singing the Lennon/McCartney-esque lyrics of "F.U." repeatedly to the sold out auditorium. Halfway through the song, I'd had enough. Something had to be done. So, I just started smashing my guitar on stage. It was about this time the flash bombs went off in the faces of Rick and our lead guitar player. There was smoke everywhere. By this time, I'd really had it, and I walked off the stage. My last words to my bandmates were: "Destroy everything!" They did! The drums were completely demolished, as well as two more guitars. They were tossing them to the stunned crowd. At this point, I ran back on stage to tear down the frame of our band sign that was hanging over where the drums were. My friend Cal, who had planned to spit out the fireball using a torch and spitting lighter fluid at it, was being held back by the organizing teacher. He managed to break free and do it. I remember him raising his arms in triumph over his accomplishment. We left the stage looking like a post-apocalyptic wasteland of what used to be a high school stage. Smoke had filled the auditorium, sprinklers had been set off over the audience. Our show was over.

The next day, we expected to be expelled. Nothing ever came of it. Some students who had friends running the contest were upset. But then something incredible happened: throughout the day, students— especially seniors—came up to me and said that was the coolest thing they'd ever seen. They also said they had my back if anyone wanted to beat me up. I went from being invisible to having bodyguards. Even though we initially thought the night was a waste, we accomplished our goal of making our mark on John Jay High. Thirty years later, no one has ever come close to topping us. It is still talked about in reverence. We are part of the school's folklore. Thankfully, no one was seriously hurt and the school did not burn down. As for me, it was like winning a gold medal on your first attempt. There was no way to top it. So, I just put it behind me and moved on. From this experience, I learned that although my niche wasn't in music, being on stage was definitely something I had an affinity for.

History:

When it came to academics, I have always had a passion for history. The first book that I ever fell in love with was *Meet George Washington* in the second grade. I must have read that book over 30 times. It got me hooked. As a kid, I would read the encyclopedia. I would read biographies for fun. Anything thing that had to do with history I would watch on TV, from the American Revolution, Civil War, the Indian Wars, and World Wars I and II. When I would watch movies on any of the topics, I would end up finding more information about them researching in the library. My dad shared the same passion and was always there to talk to me about history. He would take me to see many historical sites from Lexington and Concord, to the battlefields of Manassas. My teachers knew I had a passion for history and was always there to listen or ask questions on any subject area of history I was interested in.

History is something I wanted to share when I became teacher. I still get excited about my curriculum. My job is to share that passion. I try to keep it fresh. As a comic, I have to rework my routine to fit in today, and it's the same with teaching. I look at my lesson plans and see where I can add a twist or two that will add a little pop to my lesson. History is filled with a myriad of stories and interesting characters. I try to bring that extra dimension that sometimes the textbook fails to bring out. Every kid loves a good story, and I see myself as a humorous storyteller. My background in standup comedy has given me a tremendous edge in dealing with curriculum, classroom management, and developing relationships between students, parents, teachers, and administration.

When I got married, I decided to take my history teacher's advice and go back for my teaching certification. My wife had her degree in elementary education. Our plan was for both of us to become teachers, and I would keep doing comedy at home and go on the road on in the summers. That plan was to end when my wife taught her first class and decided to go into another profession. She wanted to become a nurse. Times were tough. She was going back to school, and I was working a civil service job: teaching a class called the *Comedy Traffic School* and doing comedy.

The *Comedy Traffic School* was a wonderful baptism into the craft of teaching. We had a curriculum and pacing guide. Somehow we had to make traffic school funny. The one thing that the people had in common was that they all wanted to be somewhere else. You had to think on your feet, so my comic skills were put to good use. My favorite part of the class was when I asked what violations the people had committed and having them tell me their stories. Most of the stories were like bad script ideas for the *Fast and the Furious* series. The traffic violators would tell the class with great pride how they were able to recklessly drive and speed 50 miles above the posted speed limit. Looking back, I think they were the actual *Fast and the Furious* scripts. I was able to improvise from the stories and still get the teaching points across. This is where I truly learned that humor and learning can go hand in hand. The class was four hours long, and gave me the confidence to pursue my career in public school teaching. It was here, in the bowels of the *Comedy Traffic School* that the Comedy/Teaching Craft was forged.

With my newfound motivation, I was eager to engage in the education coursework at the University of South Florida and was soon certified to teach middle school social studies. While back in college, one of my assignments was to visit a school and see the workings of the day to day classroom. This was an eye opener. I would see how teachers were able to, in their own way, deliver on their own style of classroom management. I asked a lot of questions and the teachers were always kind enough to spend their valuable time with me. I could not have asked for better role models. Through my observations I had bumped into an old friend, Bob Dohnal, who used to do comedy, and is still one of the top math teachers on the planet.. He introduced me to the principal, Fred Ulrich.

Fred was a wonderful man who really had the pulse on how schools really worked, and what it took to make a staff efficient. He was a straight shooter, and I respected that even if I did not agree. He would always be willing to listen. Mr. Ulrich said that there might be some job openings at the start of the next year and to put my resume in to be interviewed. I was lucky enough to get the job, and would begin teaching in the 1999-2000 school year.

"You can have the guy who likes computers, or the stand-up comic."

Those were the words that the schedule maker would ask the students going into 8th grade social studies. Of course, the serious students would pick computers and the behaviorally challenged would choose the comic. It was a "who's who" of the discipline problems of the school. This was to be my first year of teaching. I was going in the lion's den armed with my college texts and any books I could find on first year teaching. I must have bought about 10 of them. They really did not help that much. In many ways that's why I decided to write this book. I want to give my perspective, with my background as a national touring headline comedian for over 20 years, on how you can use the techniques from the stage and transfer them to the classroom. Of course, that idea did not come overnight. It took a couple of years to master the learning curve of education, and become the teacher I am today.

There is nothing like the real thing. My first year of teaching was a baptism of fire. The first thing I learned was to take care of your classroom. It's your house. I was assigned a mentor teacher to help with my first year of teaching. He saw me once. I have since tried my best when asked to help out new teachers. Administrators expect you, even as new teacher, to handle your classroom. There is no room for excuses. Did I like it? Of course not, but that's what they expected of me. I did ask the teachers for help but after I while I could still feel the agitation. So, I would have to do it on my own.

I ended up working many hours on lesson planning and coming up with strategies to stay afloat. I would find myself gravitating to the other first year teachers. We would talk about how to keep our sanity in our first year. It was like a boxing match where you are knocked down in the first minute of the first round, and now it's time to get up because there are another eleven more rounds to go. My goals were to be a professional, redraw boundaries, teach effectively, and engage the students to enjoy it.

All teachers want to be liked, but students still must respect you. That is the balance that I tried to establish with my students. I observed many different teaching styles. Some teachers would try to be the student's friend. I saw that as more of psychological deficiencies from their lost childhood. This can be a dangerous situation where the student believes they are your equal and you are crossing a fine line. There is always a distance and space that teachers should keep from their students. You can be nice. You can be an advocate. You can be a role model. But you are the authority figure in your classroom and don't ever forget that.

Some teachers, by contrast try to be incredibly intimidating. It's very old school. They are control freaks and must have everything in precise order, or their classroom with crumble like a house of cards. I've seen this work well with higher level students who have support at home and value education as a priority. To the lower level students, or students who do not get that support, they will turn off like a light switch.

Most experienced teachers would agree that parental support is one of the top indicators that will help a child make educational gains, no matter who is teaching, because those students already have built-in intrinsic motivation. Many students do not have parental support however, and the teachers of these students have to work incredibly hard to differentiate instruction for diverse learners. Yet, accountability policies at the state and local levels demand that teachers are measured and evaluated the same way. This is the big lie of our educational system. If you give me students that are chicken salad, I will give you improved chicken salad, but if you give me students that are, figuratively speaking, more like "chicken shit," I must find a way to give you back chicken salad. This, I believe is a more accurate evaluation of a highly effective teacher.

Many teachers have related that they feel a certain degree of unfairness when it comes to student placement in their schools. Often, certain teachers are given all of the brightest students. Naturally, they would do incredibly well on standardized testing and will make learning gains. Teachers of these students might brag about their prowess, but when pushed to instruct to all levels of learners they would say how they cannot deal with *"those students."* This becomes a problem for many seasoned teachers. Administration will dump the lower level and behaviorally challenged students with teachers that can handle them. While these students do not necessarily make gains on standardized test scores, they develop confidence, and commit to the learning process. It is imperative that teacher evaluation systems reflect this aspect of teaching, as opposed to relying solely on the results of a single standardized test.

I believe all teachers should have all types of students. It's the fair thing to do. It will prevent many teachers who excel with dealing with lower end students from burning out. There is just so much a teacher can give with their time and energy. In time, their flame will go out. It is more beneficial for a teacher with poor classroom management to be assigned lower level kids to actually deal with the problem and not have it passed off to a teacher that can. This is where professional development trainings come in handy.

You can never go back:

During my first year of teaching, I learned that you can never go back as a teacher. If you ever lose the classroom at the beginning of the year, it's going to be one long year. You can never get them back. It's like in poker when you show your hand and have to fold. After my first two weeks, I knew what I had done wrong. Armed with this new knowledge, I was counting the days till the next year to start over. Unfortunately, I still had to finish out my first year.

Through blood, sweat, and tears, I somehow managed to keep pushing forward. It was a struggle every day, and the key was preparation. I had to accept that each class was its own separate entity. I had to adjust my tone and actions to work with each group of students. That is how I learned about the true sense of building classroom communities. I might be teaching the same curriculum for each class, but every group is unique and had to be treated differently. It was necessary to research my students to find their deficiencies and strengths. I had to creatively move seats or change my classroom layout. I also had to use a blend of teaching and behavioral strategies.

Toward the end of my first year, I started to notice that how I prepared for, and performed, my comedy act had many parallels in the classroom. I read books on humor in the classroom and found that it could lead to gains, but what if I were to actually take everything I had learned from doing over 5000 shows and combine that with my teaching background. The Comedy/Teaching Craft was with me the whole time. While it took much work and experimentation, it was something that I was familiar with and felt comfortable doing.

So, how did I finish off my first year of teaching? I was chosen to represent my school at the Local Chamber of Commerce Tribute to Teachers. I was on my way.

PART II

Techniques of the Comedy/Teaching Craft

CHAPTER 3
THE COMEDY/TEACHING CRAFT

The Power of Stand-up:

What is so important about stand-up comedy? I want you to look in a phone book, if you still have one. If not, Google search: "brain surgeons." You will come up with quite a few names. Now, try finding someone who can hold a drunken audience's attention for an hour.

Proportionately there aren't that many. What I am saying is to be a successful stand-up comedian it takes years of hard work. It's like an apprenticeship. There are so many variables that constantly challenge a performer. No two audiences are ever alike. People are paying you to make them laugh. Many times audience members will come in with a chip on their shoulder. You can't wait for the next show. It's up to you to deal with it. That's how you grow.

My goal in comedy is to make it seem so easy that anyone from the audience can say: "He just walked up on stage and started being funny." Nothing can be farther from the truth than that. The preparation that goes into creating an act is an ever-changing process that takes years to develop. The first step in becoming a professional comic is to becoming an M.C. (master of ceremonies) or opening act, where your job is to warm up the crowd with a mixture of material and breaking the comedic ice. It's very challenging to go up on stage cold. You have to read the audience instantly and steer the act in that direction. This takes time. There are obstacles of people talking, cell phones, people eating, getting settled, or just not paying attention. So, by the time I get off the stage, the audience, which came in as a fragmented disjointed group, has been brought together by laughter. To become a good M.C., and to be versatile enough to work with many groups, takes about three years. Good M.C.'s are tough to come by today, because everyone wants to skip this step and do their act from the get-go. They forget the most important part of a show in bringing the audience together.

I had the fortune of learning to M.C. at the *Last Laff* in San Jose, California. I would play to audiences of over 200 people, for 6 nights a week, with incredible comics with resumes and television credits. A job like that helps you develop, and the owners expect you to be good. After a while, if you cannot handle the duties of and M.C., you are let go. Comedy can be cruel.

Moving up from M.C., your next goal is to become a feature act. The feature act is the comic who comes on after the M.C. and before the headliner. As the "comic in the middle," they are required to do 25-30 minutes. They usually have a structured act from beginning to the end. Many comics feel the feature spot is the easiest to succeed. They don't have to waste time performing M.C. duties, and can just hit the stage strong. The pressure of closing a show (often felt by the headliner) is not there. Therefore, your mind is now free to relax and evaluate material, and even improvise if you want. Because of this, the feature act can sometimes be the funniest person on the show.

How do you come up with your comedy set?

When I was starting out, another comic shared Judy Carter's (1989) method of comedic set development. First, I'd assign numbers to my best comedic bits in descending order from 1-10, (with number 1 being your strongest). I then set up my performance by taking bits 1, 3, 5, 7, 9, and then follow with bits 10, 8, 6, 4, 2. The goal was to come up with a consistent set that would open strong and close strong. Too many times, comics will just use their best material up front, and then burn out like a candle. By designing my set through weaving my material, I don't run the risk of losing the audience, and having them shut down on me. If I follow a joke that doesn't go well with another downer, my set could start spiraling down the comedic toilet bowl. By weaving my set, I ensure the opposite. I get laughs, hold the audience's attention and I maintain the comfort and confidence to know my material is going to get stronger laughs as I end.

Moving from feature to headliner can take any amount of time. A headlining act is someone who can do a solid 45 minute- to an hour-length show. The headliner makes the most money and has the pressure of being the last person on stage. Thus, if the other two previous acts fail it is up to the headliner to make sure the show goes well and the audience goes home happy. Even though there might be an array of distractions going on in the club, the club owner expects no excuses from a headliner who does not do well.

Preparation H: How do you prepare for being a Headlining Act?

I got my start at headlining after years of being a feature act that would outperform the headliner. Club owners became aware of this and eventually began to headline me at the lower level clubs. It was great way to learn the ropes as I moved up to bigger clubs and venues.

Like good teaching, good headlining takes real preparation. I make sure to get rest so that my brain is sharp and ready for anything. I am a creature of routine. If I have time, I take a nap to get rested. I'll have an early dinner. I don't like to have a full stomach when I'm on stage. For some reason, I think it restricts me.

I always write an outline of my set, which takes about 25 minutes. First, I review the comedic premises, or main topics, that I'll perform for the audience. From each premise, I have several tangents that I could explore if I see that the audience responds well to a particular premise. My goal is to craft a set that will appeal to and perform well for all groups, from young professionals, to retirees. I must be prepared for any audience. After I write my set, I will turn the TV on and take my time dressing. This helps to clear my mind and transition to the mental state that it takes to be on stage. It's a quiet reflection time that provides me with the confidence to know whatever the challenge is, I will be prepared.

When I arrive at a club, I always check in with whoever's in charge to go over the time schedules and see if there is anything that I could do to help them out, outside of my act. It's important for me to build relationships with the owners, so they will not only say: "You were funny," but also: "You're easy to work with," and they'd "be happy to rebook" me.

I always observe and assess the audience before I hit the stage. I want to know who I am performing to. I ask the hostess if there any large groups or celebrations, so I can prepare a couple of lines that will draw them into my show. I ask for any local references that will further endear me to the audience. I want them to feel that I am not a canned act, but a performer who has personalized the show for this audience. It makes a great deal of difference in the audience's perception of me. My goal is to lead the audience, and not the other way around.

When the show starts, I watch the acts that precede me intently. I have to gauge the audience and see if the comic is doing well or not. I have to see what type of humor they are laughing at, and if the acts are clean or dirty. It's very tough to go clean when the acts before me have been dirty. The feature may be doing material on graphic sexual situations, and trust me, once that door has been opened, it's really tough to close it. The audience now expects me to top it, not to talk about the cute things that my kids did this summer. As the headliner,

I've to be able to change the tone and content of my act in an instant. That is what being a professional all is about.

I watch the other acts to see if any of my premises have been covered. If this happens, I have to alter my bit, or just take it out of my act. I also try to watch the previous acts to see if there is any part of their performance that I might be able to come up with something funny or use as a bridge when I get to the stage. Jumping into my set right away can seem way too contrived and when I transition by talking about some things from the previous acts the audience knows that you are in the moment, and funny enough to play off something I just heard. They get the perception right away: "This guy is sharp." He listens. He knows what's going on in the club and in the area. This buys good will with the audience, lets them know that I am funny, and they will give me the benefit of the doubt and pay attention. That is all a comic can ask for! I know it's up to me to bring it home to the audience.

After each set, I reflect on what went well, and what could have gone better. Reflection is a key part of growth. If one learns to reflect and take constructive criticism on how to improve their act, even after 20 years, it's going to provide added longevity to a career.

So, the next time you see a comic on stage, you should be able to tell how prepared he was for the show. You are now aware that when you go to a comedy club and see a comic look like it's all rolling off the top of his tongue, that in reality there has been a tremendous about of experience and hard work that has been put into his act. If you perceive that the comic just made it up, and was having a good time, then the comic has done their job.

The Stand-up/Teacher Connection:

If while reading, you have noticed that a lot of what is done in stand-up comedy parallels what you have done as a teacher, then you're right. There are so many strategies and techniques used on the stage that teachers perform variations of every day. That is the core of what this book is about!

- Fact: There is an incredible connection that cannot be denied between how comedians engage their audiences and how teachers engage their students.

- Fact: There is a massive connection between the time both comedians and teachers spend in preparation of their routines and lesson plans.

- Fact: There is also a huge connection between comedians and teachers when it comes to reflection and revision.

- Fact: This is the first book of its kind in history to bring together not just humor and teaching, but the art of stand-up comedy and teaching.

- Fact: It has taken me twenty-five years of working as a nationally touring, headlining comedian, and award-winning teacher to bring this practical, no-nonsense perspective together. You can only find it here.

The Rivera Teaching Soapbox:

I truly believe it takes a number of years to grasp the art of teaching. Your teaching style should always be evolving. We are lifelong learners. Keeping your mind open is the key. Many teachers, including myself at times, retreat to the safety of "teaching comfort zones." This will only stymie ideas and strategies that could potentially have validity to them. Ego is the barrier between being a good teacher and becoming a great teacher. I don't want wake up one morning, only realize through my own selfish pride that I could have done more to improve my craft as an educator. My students, and the world, deserve better.

So, how would I describe my teaching style? The real question is: How would my students describe my teaching style? After all, they are the ones who are with me every day. I remember one student said that I was like "a big kid who was their teacher." I like to have fun in classroom. It's part of who I am. I have been a professional stand-up comedian for over 20 years. It has to influence the way I teach. I do think I am unique. I have been able to bring what I have done in front of audiences and adapt it with success into the classroom. Research shows that humor positively contributes to the level of engagement in the classroom. According to Marzano (2007):

> *Mokowitz and Hayman (1976) "found that the most effective junior high teachers tended to joke with students and smiled frequently" (p. 153). Also, Gettinger and Koher (2006) noted that when teachers project a positive and enthusiastic demeanor, students are likely to adopt the same general stance in class. Moreover, Bettencort, Gillet, Gall and Hull (1983) found that teachers showing enthusiasm had positive effects on "student engagement and achievement" (p. 153).*

People ask: How was I able to go from becoming a nationally touring headline comedian to an award winning stand-up teacher? The answer is simple: I was able to incorporate my mastery of stand-up comedy and transfer it into the classroom. Did it come overnight? No, but it's been a valuable skill that I knew I would be able translate to the classroom over the past 15 years.

Do you have to be a stand-up comedian to use my techniques and strategies? No. but I can help you find your own way to "bring the funny out in you." I will now empower you with secrets of the Comedy/Teaching Craft.

The STAND-UP Teacher:

My goal is for you to become a Stand-Up Teacher.

- Stand-up in the sense that you will have the knowledge and the techniques to captivate the students in your classroom, just like a comic does for a live audience.

- Stand-up in the sense that you will raise the bar in your own personal development as a professional educator by incorporating strategies that will result in gains for all stakeholders.

- Stand-up to rise above common pitfalls or to rekindle your passion to teach that led you pick up this book.

STAND-UP is the acronym for:
S: START your engines
T: TIMING Take a breath, take a break
A: AWARENESS of your surroundings
N: NOW is the time, (Be in the NOW)
D: DROP the dead weight
U: USE the kitchen sink
P: PHONEY baloney

Each strategy will be broken into 7 categories:

1. What problems are you having in the classroom?
2. What problem parallels this classroom problem in comedy?
3. How do I solve the problem in comedy?
4. How would you transfer this solution to the classroom?
5. Practical classroom examples.
6. Review Steps.
7. Reflection Questions.

CHAPTER 4

FIVE FOUNDATIONS OF CLASSROOM MANAGEMENT

AKA: "DO THIS OR YOU WILL DIE."

None of the advice that I can give you will be helpful unless you master a few key aspects of classroom teaching. Before you can stand-up, you need a foundation to stand on.

The behavior plan is the cornerstone of every classroom. If successful, it will make your school year a whole lot easier. If not, you can feel like you are trapped in quicksand from the first week of class, to the end of the year.

You can never have a do-over from the beginning of the year as a teacher. The first priority is to show students that there is a certain line that will never be crossed in the classroom. Your rules, procedures, consequences, and boundaries must be clear.

Rules and Procedures:

I have a simple set of rules in my class. It's the minimum set of expectations that have to be met so that I can teach, and the students can learn. For example, when I'm giving the class directions, students must listen. They should be free of distractions. Do I demand silence at all times? Of course not! They can talk while working in groups, or during transitions between activities. I have learned to pick my battles. Human beings are social, whether it is in the comedy club or in the classroom. I just have to work around it. That said, instructional time is sacred in my classroom. I communicate my rules and procedures at the beginning of the year, and review them after each grading period. Just as you figure out your style in comedy, you have to figure out your own set of class expectations. Every teacher has a different level of tolerance. You want to keep your rules list short, easy for them to follow, and easy for you to enforce.

Consequences & Consistency:

Are kids always going to be on task? Of course not, and you must correct them. But what happens when one of your top students is off task repeatedly? At first you want to give them the benefit of the doubt, but you realize that the whole class is watching. I always tell the students: "The rules apply to everyone or they don't apply at all." There are times when even I have to call a student out for violating the class rules. The student is shocked because they believe they have earned enough credibility for me to let it slide. I tell them what they did is wrong, and then I hit them with the question: "Do the rules apply to all?" This gives them pause, and gets them thinking. Now, they are the center of attention, and since they are smart, they know the best thing to do is to say "Yes" to diffuse the situation. Some would call it a "Jedi Mind Trick," I just call it good teaching. Notice that I did not yell or embarrass the student. Not only does this model proper behavior, it also demonstrates emotional control. The rest of the class gets it: in Mr. Rivera's classroom, everyone is equal, and if boundary is crossed, there are consequences. Students that can be behavior problems really notice this, and are more likely to buy in to your classroom dynamics. Now, when I prompt them with: "The rules apply to all..." the whole class now responds: "...or they don't apply at all!"

Boundaries:

As I've mentioned earlier, everyone wants to be liked, and it's great when a class enjoys you and the way you teach. As we set boundaries for students we must always put boundaries on ourselves as teachers. Are we authority figures and role models? Yes, but first and foremost, we are teachers. There are certain boundaries teachers must never cross with students. I'm not talking about the obvious ones that are in the paper every week. I'm talking about the boundary that exists between the roles of teacher and student. I've seen teachers cross the line by taking the popular, intelligent, or advanced students and making them into friends. They overstep by sharing campus gossip about other students and even other teachers. Who does that really benefit? Is it the student, or the teacher with the fragile ego, that needs validation from their students?

Yes, some of the more popular teachers among students are like that. What they did not get as a child in school or cannot get as an adult now, manifests as an inappropriate emotional relationship. On the surface, it may look like a teacher taking a few special students under their wing. In reality, it is a major red flag that could have Professional Standards knocking on the door. I have a rule: if you can't say it to your whole class and to your administrative staff, you don't say it at all. This is even true for "America's Most Hilarious Teacher."

I always keep my door open for two reasons: first, it is to invite anyone passing by to hear what is going on in my classroom, and the other is to show that I have nothing to hide. I am a funny teacher but I'm also a professional. Keep it black and white when it comes to the boundary between student and teacher.

Congratulations! If you have mastered these concepts, you are already on your way to becoming a STAND-UP teacher.

MIKE RIVERA

PART III
The STAND-UP Strategies

CHAPTER 5
"S:" START YOUR ENGINES

Classroom Problem:

How many times have you started your lesson plan only to realize that after two minutes your students are in a vegetative state? They are quiet, but also completely tuned out. If your lesson had an EKG attached, it would be flat lining. Unless something is done "STAT," the patient will be dead, and so will your lesson. Because the class is quiet, you mistake that for attentiveness. I can't tell you how many times, when I was a student, I would be bored to death. I mastered the art of nodding and keeping my eyes on the board to make the teacher think I was enthralled in their lesson. In reality, I was off on some tropical island thousands of miles away.

You think your lesson is going well until you call out for an answer, and the students don't know where you're at. Pick on the students that are nodding their heads. Hopefully, they will not ask you to bring them a Pina colada and sun umbrella as I did. More than likely, they will ask you to repeat the question, or they just give you a blank stare. They ask:

"What page are we are on?" You assume that just because this lesson is part of the curriculum standards, it should be good enough. While it's good enough for you, the teacher, it is torture to the student. Upon reflection, you realize that you are educational version of the Marquis De Sade... or the villain from *Saw*.

Comedy Problem:

In comedy you have to start strong. You need that hook from the start or it's going to be a long night. Your comedy career will be over before it gets started. You can only make one first impression. People have short attention spans and can tune you out in a minute, so it's important to let them know you are funny from the start. Once you have them on the hook, you can be effective. You also need to end strong to leave that lasting impression. Just as in a good political speech, they will remember you from the start and the finish. If you have a weak ending it sometimes damages the impression of the entire set.

Comedy Solution:

When I come out on stage to a cold room, I will hit the audience with a few quick one liners from my set, or I'll improvise lines that I know will fit based on how the show's been going. I will not waste time giving a long setup and punchline. I go for the throat, because that what it takes today. In comedy you are always one minute away from someone checking Facebook.

I was doing a show at a local Veterans of Foreign Wars (VFW) post, which is not normally a comedy hotbed. There were about 150 people there, and the average age was about 65. The room was like a gigantic basement from *That 70's Show*. I knew right away I would hit them with jokes about "reverse mortgages," "nighttime meds," and anything covered in the AARP manual. I was able to make fun of their Bingo machine by saying: "Don't worry... If I bomb, we can always play bingo." I also kept it clean without cursing as to not to offend them. Within five minutes, I had broken the ice and won them over. By the end of the show, they had prepared a ham dinner plate for me to take back to my hotel room.

Transfer to the Classroom:

Teachers also have to win over the students within the first couple of minutes. Today, it's called getting "street credibility" (a.k.a. "street cred"), which means you've earned their respect. If you have watched *Dangerous Minds*, or *8 Mile*, you know that getting street cred is no easy task. You have to make an effort to show that you care. You must gain an understanding of who they are, and what their lives are like. Lessons have to be relevant to their culture and/or socioeconomic status, or it's "peace out, dude." In the past, students would automatically give teachers respect. Parents would always back up the teachers at home. Today, it doesn't work that way. If you're able to reach out to the student in a culturally relevant way, it will make all the difference. Many teachers, out of stubbornness or failure to adapt to the times, refuse to reach out. Well, welcome to a new day. If you don't have the cred, you won't get in their head.

Classroom Example:

During the first couple of days, I establish my boundaries, and then I take some time to get to know the kids, and let them get to know each other. Many books on education call this team building, establishing a class culture, or breaking the ice. The purpose of this exercise is to "gain intel" on the situation to guide your decision-making.

I start out by giving a frank and honest introduction of myself. Many students will come into your classroom with a preconceived notion of who you are. I want to be the one who tells them about me. After my introduction, I tell my students that they may always challenge me if I ever break my word to them. They have permission to call me out even if they believe I have broken any of the set of rules that I set out for myself. They are caught off guard, but it sets the stage that we are all in this together. It communicates that we are all stakeholders.

Next, I give a climate survey to the kids. I put a heavy emphasis on popular culture. I want to know what they're into and research it. Topics could include: movies, music, video games, hobbies, sports, YouTube streams, or other interests. I don't want to seem outdated or like I'm trying to be cool—I already know that I'm cool. The students are always honest and blunt in their responses. It requires much time and effort on my part to go through them, but it's well worth it. Any nugget you find to connect with a student is priceless. In class, I will start making references from their surveys. The students will either laugh or smile, and so will you, because you are hooking them in.

Being a father of a two middle school children has been an eye-opener. My son started the 6th grade extremely shy and withdrawn. He would confide in me that he felt alone and different from the rest of the students. I could imagine that he was not the only student who felt that way. Thus, I added two questions to my 8th grade Climate Survey. The first was: "Do you ever feel alone at school?" The second was: "Do you think you are different from the rest of the students?" To my surprise, over 60 percent of my students often answer "yes" to both questions. I share this percentage with my classes. They are surprised to hear the results, but are relieved to know that there are many that think the way they do. So, instead of feeling different and alone, they now know they are in the mainstream. I use this as a teachable moment in class. Middle school, and all new transitions in life, can difficult. It's my goal in teaching to facilitate both academic and social growth. I am Mr. Thackeray.

Finally, I give a baseline assessment that is three to four grades below them. The purpose is to identify those students that have been left behind. These are students who will need the extra help that have IEPs (Individualized Education Plans for students with special needs), and special accommodations. I am always surprised how many students have fallen through cracks of the educational gulag. Now, instead of waiting to hear from the behavior specialist for instructions and accommodations, I can begin right away. I can start building my classroom dynamics with picture that is clearer, and less stressful for students and myself.

Day to Day:

Once I've built my initial street cred by getting to know my students and showing them that I am a caring adult in their lives, the rest is day to day maintenance. I start by observing my students as they are walking into to the classroom. Many students express their emotions outwardly through body language. They may arrive at my door with shoulders slumped, tears in their eyes, or occasionally in "*Full Hulk Mode*" when they slam their books on the floor.

The goal is, by the time the bell rings, to have the temperature of the classroom already gauged. So, now my job is to warm them up like an opening act. If there has been a difficult test in Math, I will mention it to them. If someone has a frown on their face, I will ask them "What's going on?" I acknowledge any celebrations, sporting victories, or schoolwide functions. If there is a hot topic that has been buzzing around the school campus, I'm going to bring it up. I always remember to keep my comments appropriate and professional. One thing the students love is to talk about an issue that concerns them. Students will always have an opinion and love to share it. I was on *The View* three times: they always start their show with what is happening in the world right now. It's the same for students. Once class starts, I am like radar operator making room sweeps to make sure the class is all on the same page. They are ready because I showed that I cared what was going on in the moment. The transition is now smoother because they are at ease. The students see me as a real person and worthy of a place in their circle of trust. Now that I have their trust, they are hooked and ready to learn.

During lesson planning I will put a huge emphasis on my hook. Just as in comedy, a good hook is both auditory and visual. You'd be surprised how excited students can get when they see the *YouTube* logo on the projector screen or SMART Board. It's keyed into our students' brains. I also use current events and articles from the news. Try an outlet like

CNN Student News or *TIME for Kids*, since the articles are written with the student audience in mind. The classroom isn't the VFW, but it doesn't have to be *The New York Times* either. Remember: You have to play to your audience.

Keep your hook short, and no more than three minutes. Every Monday morning, I know that most of my kids have watched *The Walking Dead*. The students can't wait to have our own version of *The Talking Dead*. We spend no more than three minutes on this discussion. We live in the age of Twitter, and the kids realize the power of keeping questions and answers short. When we are done, all I have to say is: "Let's start the day." I have my street cred. We are ready to go.

Keeping kids interested in events that happened in the 18th and 19th centuries can be challenging. For example, I was doing a lesson on the causes of the American Revolution. The History Channel had an incredible three-minute review of it. Why was it effective? They use slow motion, CGI, and it's exciting. It gave kids a rush that they don't expect to see or hear in the classroom. As we know from TV news: "If it bleeds, it leads," but I always use my judgment as a professional. The key is to think outside the box and get that "wow" moment. Once you do that, they're yours. An added benefit to a good hook, or an exciting lesson, is that now you have something to draw the student's attention back during future lessons.

Review Steps:

1. It's essential in comedy, and teaching, to gain and maintain your audience's attention.
2. Start the year with the goal of gaining street cred from your students. Work on maintaining it each day.
3. Maintain your cred by discussing and mentioning examples from pop culture, such as movies, TV shows, current events, and hot topics in school.
4. Find out what the students are talking about in halls and bring it into to class. Keep it appropriate, and remember the boundaries.

Reflection Questions:

1. How do you build and maintain positive relationships by getting to know your students at the beginning of the year?
2. How can you gain a better understanding of your student's interests? What questions can you ask them?
3. How do you hook students, and establish "street cred" to encourage student buy-in?

CHAPTER 6
"T:" TIMING: THE YO-YO EFFECT

Classroom Problem:

Have you ever finished a lesson or class period and noticed that the students were popping in and out of the lesson? There was an inconstancy level in their engagement. You felt as though they only got bits and pieces of the lesson. During times in the lesson, you felt they were eating from the palm of your hand, but ten minutes later you realized that they would rather be eating in the cafeteria. You have now experienced the **Yo-Yo effect** of teaching.

Comedy Problem:

Many times, even after a good performance, I've felt like the audience's attention span varied: sometimes they were with me, but other times I'd lost them. It's the same act that I had been doing for years, with tried and true material. This often gave me cause to reflect on what went wrong. Having an okay set that gets consistent laughter, but doesn't bring the house down, might cause one to think that the audience was a bit tight. However, too many highs and lows is a red flag. Once you get a level of laughter, you have to sustain it. Your job is to keep the party going.

Comedy Solution:

For yo-yo audiences, you have to figure out how to manage your energy. Some comics draw energy from the previous comic. This is no problem if the comic they follow did well, but how will they adjust when they have to follow a comic who just bombed?

Effective comics know how to manage the energy of the room, and sustain it for their entire set. If they know that they are going up to a dead audience, a comic can capture that level with a combination of crowd work, topical issues, and a strong, confident delivery. Comics don't ask the audience if it's funny. Their demeanor on stage tells them that it is funny. They manage their volume and tempo, picking up when the audience needs to take a breath and slow down. They have to infuse passion and energy into each individual joke and story in their act as if they are telling it for the first time.

I'm on stage for 45 minutes to an hour, which is about the same duration as a class period. I know the pace of my show has to be consistent. This involves analyzing my act and keeping it strong from beginning to end. There are no "slow songs" in comedy. Each new topic in the act has to have the same punch and energy level that I open with, otherwise it's back to the yo-yo effect. A comic is the conductor of a comedy train. The audience members are passengers. Once I get them on board, I keep the train moving forward, and the passengers don't get off until I let them. My transitions between topics are key to keeping everyone from jumping off at the next stop (and start texting). Sometimes you have to slow it down to pick up the stragglers who don't get it, because your job is to get all passengers to their laughter destination. You have to bring it, and differentiate to everyone.

In comedy clubs, I average playing to crowds of 150-200. It is important to play the whole room. I don't want anyone to feel left out. In my pre-show observations, I look for people that I will be able to use as my "anchors." My comedy anchors are people from each section of the audience. Through years of shows, I have developed comic instincts,

I know who will be willing to go along with my playful banter. They are my audience allies and have my back. Throughout my act, I have built in areas where I can label a member of the audience with a name that coincides with material I'm performing. I have bits on Hank Hill, turtles, stoners, and Bullwinkle the Moose. They love it, and feel a part of the show, as do the people who are in their section. The labeled audience member becomes a "group leader" for that section. If I feel I am not getting a good response from a section, I will include the comedy anchors in the next bit to punch up the section. At the end of the show they will inevitably always come up to me with members in their section saying: "I was Hank," "I was the turtle," "I was the stoner," or "I was the Moose." They leave the club happy, and I leave the club with the invitation to return.

Transfer to the Classroom:

Just like a comedic set, teachers have to learn how to pace their classes. If I have two shows a night, in-between shows I give myself some sort of down time where I can get my head together. At the comedy club you get a half hour, but at school it is just a few minutes. I take a minute to sit down close my eyes and decompress the events of last period and get myself ready for the next class. The key is I am taking the time to shut down and start fresh or my day runs the risk of becoming a seven-hour marathon (of *Mad Men*).

After my minute, I focus on the next group of students. They are my main concern. I will call out their names and mention the class period number. This reminds me, that for the students, it's the first time they have seen me all day. It gives me an energy boost, so that I can convey their importance to me. I am aware of my energy level and ready for the class. The class is not going to get that I have been sapped of energy from the daily rigor of teaching. The goal is to give them a fresh teacher. Again, the talented professionals make this look easy.

My awareness of the changing student dynamics can be used to make each class transition as smooth as possible. If I see the class is tired or down, I know I'm going to have to be a little loud and lift the mood of the room. If the class is rowdy, I need to settle the students down. It's a mistake to ignore energy and emotion as the students as they arrive, but it's also a mistake to get the students worked up and send them on to the next teacher, who will have to deal with kids who are rowdy and overcharged. When I took control of my energy level, I was able to break the day into manageable segments. This decreased stress, and allowed me to handle classroom problems without feeling overwhelmed. At the end of each day, I had energy left over to focus on my family and my health.

Classroom Example:

Let's imagine, in a seven-period day, I have six classes per day, and an additional class period reserved for planning. As far as my day goes, I know that the classes that require more hands on attention are periods one, three, and seven. The first two have a lower level learners, which requires me to differentiate my instruction to suit them. The last class of the day is always a challenge. It really doesn't matter what level of learners you have. This class has most likely mentally vacated the premises.

As students come in to my class for 7th period, I am already working the room with lines like "You made it, one more to go, hang in there, we can do it!" They're tired, and they know I feel the same way. In between my acknowledgements about the time of day, I'm reminding them of the agenda for the day and how important it is to complete. Even though it's always posted on my board, telling them about it gives them a sense of urgency that we still have a job to do. They are now aware that once the lesson or assignment is over; it's time to go home. For this reason, when compared to my other classes, this group often gets the lesson done the fastest.

For my classes in the beginning of the day, that require more hands on attention, I always go over what supplies and what they are going to need to get the class going. I stress the importance with a smile. I take my time to make sure everyone is ready to learn. I am totally aware that I will have to repeat directions. During work time, I circulate the room more frequently for maintaining attention to their task. I have some students working at my front table. Now to some kids, it might not seem cool to be working at the teachers table, but I make it worth it to them. The "front-table kids" get classroom privileges, breaks, and rewards, but they know they are expected to do the work. I will also joke around with them to put them at ease. The result is that the kids are getting the required attention. The work is being done. Finally, I am the one who is controlling the pace of the class. The yo-yo effect has been averted.

Review:

1. Take breaks between classes to decompress and recharge.
2. Evaluate student moods as they come in to class in order to make "gauge the temperature" of the incoming class.
3. Establish and reinforce a routine for the beginning of each class.
4. Make sure the whole class is with you and prepared to learn before you begin the content your lesson.
5. Look for cues during your lesson as to when elevate your energy level, then follow through.
6. For students that need extra attention, find creative ways to engage them.

Reflection Questions:

1. How do you manage your energy level during the school day?
2. How do you gauge the energy level of your students and channel it in positive ways?
3. How do you prevent the yo-yo effect, or deal with changing energy levels of your students?

CHAPTER 7
"A:" AWARENESS

Classroom Problem:

At the beginning of every school year, I will always find out that some or many students are going to be behavioral challenges. It can be a variety of things: they can talk out in class, they can be disrespectful to the teacher and fellow students, they can be tuned out, and so on. Chances are they going to be taken out of your class by administration. You don't have to be a rocket scientist to figure out that one out. Of course, I already have my class rules set up. To some students the rules are merely suggestions. In the beginning, one might think this behavior must be an act, but after a while you realize this is the student's real persona. As teachers, we must begin working on behavior remediation immediately.

Comedy Problem:

The first thing I do when I go into a comedy club is to size up the room. I'm looking for potential problems. Like a good boy scout, a comic is always prepared. I like to see if there are tables that are already drunk. Do I see any serial texters? Are there any celebrations? Do I see any large birthday parties, or bachelorette parties? Are there people from out of town? Is there a company party going on? Also, I might notice that the audience is quiet. All of these are potential land mines that can go off during your show. It is my job to make them go away as quickly as possible without seriously disrupting the comedy performance.

Comedy Solution:

It's all about making the first move. It just takes a few minutes. I can talk with manager or someone from the wait staff that can fill me in on some information from each group. The goal is to already have a humorous line waiting for them. I don't try to confront or belittle them, or I may turn an entire section of my audience against me. So, when I give a line a say it with a smile. I give them a shout of praise and then I zing them. It might take a couple of times but they feel like, hey the comic is making an attempt to reach us in a fun way. We like him. He is one of us.

For the comic's part, it's not a major catastrophe waiting to happen. It comes with the territory of performing to audiences. My job is to be the professional who has experience dealing with diverse crowds. It's all pop psychology. I have to make a quick diagnosis and have an action plan already to go. Many times it's just a change in demeanor that can be the key to a great show. I can't have my show being taken over by groups or hecklers (see Chapter 13 for more advice on dealing with hecklers). I have the microphone. It's up to me to get the job done. Can it be stressful? Yes, but that's why club owners are paying me.

Bachelorette parties are always a potential time bomb. They are all dressed up with silly attire and have gifts that just crave attention. The successful comic will balance out compliments with jokes. I weave in my material on getting married, honeymoons, and engagement rings. The group now believes I have just written material just for them. I was going to use it anyway, but I make it look that it is customized for them. My goal is to have them believe that I am a part of their group. We have bonded. It works, and most of the time when a large party comes they will invite me to go out with them after the show, or ask to friend me on Facebook so that they can come back and see me the next time I am in town.

There are times when I will have the terminal groups of hecklers. Since I go up last in a three-person show, I have the opportunity to watch how the audience is behaving. If I see any real potential for disaster, then I will talk to the manager of the club. I will discuss options that can be done by the staff. I tell the manager to watch me and look for any code words or phrases that I have pre-planned that then will ask the management to step in and deal with situation. It doesn't happen that often, but it's all about not being blindsided and making that first move before the show. The staff and management will appreciate it, which in turn will get you a good evaluation. It seems like everyone is being evaluated today. Comics are no different, and there is little room for error.

Transfer to the Classroom:

So, how do I make the first move and reach out to diverse groups of students? I am aware that this is a problem for many, especially new teachers. Often, new teachers feel as if they are on their own. It's like the educational version of *Survivor*. They are dropped into classroom with the barest of essentials. It's up to them, not only survive, but to succeed in the educational process of their students.

Part of "gaining my intel" is that I start each year by taking my roster down to the previous grade level. I show it the teachers, the counselors, and administrators. They put a check by any possible behavioral or motivationally challenged student and make other notes that are so helpful throughout the year. Now, here is the key: Do not believe that every student that is checked is going to be a challenge. It is just a guide for you so that you are not caught blindsided. It also helps with making seating charts at the beginning of the year, which you can always change. After the first week, you should have a good idea where any potential problems are going to come from.

Now, I try to be as prepared as I can be when school starts and have intel on possible disruptions. Sometimes they will never manifest, but if they do, I'm prepared. A key benefit of this level of preparation is that your reaction will be less volatile than the reactions of the other teachers.

Many times I will see a student come into my classroom in an agitated state. This can be a time bomb waiting to explode, but I will not let it happen in my classroom. If a student is agitated and upset, it most likely from something that has just happened during the day. As soon as I see this I will quietly and ask the student if something is wrong. Of course something is wrong, but I'm giving them a way to tell me. I always give students options. If they feel better talking to the guidance counselor, I will send them out, or even better, if the student has a friend in the classroom that they feel comfortable with to talk with, I give them four minutes to take the pass and discuss the situation. The problem comes back diffused and witnessed by the entire class where my street credibility has just gone way up. You're now the teacher version of *MacGyver*: you keenly assessed the situation and quickly diffused the situation.

Guilt is Your Friend:

One of the basic tools I learned from my mother as a kid, being raised Catholic; my mother would always use guilt as a way to make me feel bad. In the classroom, I have been able to use guilt as my friend.

So, yes, guilt can be a wonderful thing when used in a positive manner. Often at the beginning of the year, I hear about one of my students beginning to misbehave in other classes, and has shown warning signs of in my classroom. My master plan involves patience, kindness, and most of all: a healthy dose of guilt. Guilt in the fact that I know, within the first week, and that every other teacher has been having a problem with the student, but I was prepared and showed patience. I made the first move with an act of kindness. Of course, I do not let them cross boundaries, and I have kept my cool. Remember, passive aggressive behavior cannot be met with similar behavior in return. That is what the student wants, and has experienced in the past. I keep a smile on when they have a little flare up in my class, and they will be caught off guard. That can be so frustrating to the student who is used to being treated one way. Now, the student is the one who is blindsided by my behavior. That's when I can work at having them adjust their disruptions. So where does guilt factor in?

Classroom Example:

At the beginning of the year I had a student who was not aware of how I ran things. Students love to test boundaries to see how much they can get away with. The student was acting up in class. I told the student to wait till after class. I told the student how their behavior was inappropriate. I asked what they expected to happen. They expected to be written up and sent to the principal's office. I made it clear to them that my job is not to be their adversary, but to be their advocate and as long as they tried their best, I would be on their side. Of course, I knew all about the student and problems they have had last year. All the teachers and administrators had been talking about the student. I knew for a fact that the student in their present frame of mind would be written up by multiple teachers. I was unsurprised to find out that they were.

The next time I saw the student I asked how they have been. I had already known they had in-school suspension. They student told me what had happened. Of course, I had to ask the student: "Who was the only teacher that gave them the benefit of the doubt, and cut you a break?" They said: "It was you, Mr. Rivera." So yes, guilt can be a wonderful thing when used in a positive manner. It was the spark that was needed to have the student start buying into me as a teacher, and my class. Did the student act up again in my class? Of course, but the rate and time of class disruptions dwindled. After about six weeks, the student was trying. The student did require assistance. I sat him with students who were good at providing positive peer support. By the end of the year, the student had a "C" average. It's wasn't an "A," but it was the best he could do. I was happy and could go on to the next student. By making that first move, I was able to preemptively solve a potential problem. As teachers we have our lesson plans, but we should always have a special "master plan" ready and handy in our back pocket.

Warning: You don't have to be a hero. Nobody is perfect. This is not a movie where at the end every student ends up loving the teacher. Go with your instinct. You know when you have exhausted all resources. At this point, find out if there are any classes where the student is being successful, and ask the teacher for their take on the situation. That's what professional learning communities are for. Three minutes talking with another teacher can end up being the biggest investment of your school year. If it's still a problem, talk to your grade level guidance counselor. More than likely, they're going to be aware of the situation. They may be able to offer possible solutions or interventions. Only after exhausting all resources will I go to my grade level administrator. Let's be real, the less time they have to deal with disruptive students the better for them and for you. Remember, if you can keep anecdotal records of everything you have done, it will soften any potential negative impact on you and your abilities with classroom management.

Review Steps:

1. You will have to develop and hone the skills to deal with disruptions in the classroom.
2. Research the student's academic and behavioral records. Take time to look over any IEPs or accommodation plans, and create a notecard or folder on the student. If it's a new student have your data prep clerk call the old school and get all the records transferred.
3. Channel your inner *MacGyver* by preemptive diffusion as opposed to damage control.
4. Remember negative attention is still attention. The key is the teacher's reaction. You have to maintain control over the situation to get that breakthrough moment with the student. Be like *Horse Whisperer* or just use my mother's "master plan" of guilt. You are the adult, and can manipulate the situation to benefit your classroom dynamics.

Reflection Questions:

1. What steps do you currently take to become aware of the potential challenges and individual needs of your students?
2. What is your behavior plan for dealing with the most disruptive situations?
3. Think of a time when you were unable to preemptively solve a problem. What was your demeanor, and what was the result? How could you have changed your reaction to attain a more positive outcome?

CHAPTER 8
"N:" NOW IS THE TIME. BE IN THE MOMENT

Classroom Problem:

There have been times when I thought I came up a with a great lesson plan, only to see it work for certain classes and falter in others. I created what I believed was a brilliant way to teach the contentious Election of 1800, between the Federalists, led by Alexander Hamilton, and the Republicans led by Thomas Jefferson. The campaign could rival any of the mud-slinging of today's elections. My hook was to play the highly partisan campaign songs of each political party. I believed the students would see this as a 19th Century version of a rap battle, without the microphone drop. After engaging the students with the songs, I would then get into the nuts and bolts of the Election. The lesson went beautifully for my first 3 classes. When I got to my 4th period class, to my amazement, I could hear a pin drop. Mechanically I was there. I was doing the lesson that "killed" for the first three classes. I knew this inconsistency had to be addressed. I could not wait until tomorrow. It had to be done for the next class or even better yet, during that class. My students were tuning me out and channel surfing in their brains. At this point to save the lesson, I had to look at what I could do to change the dynamics of the instruction immediately.

Comedy Problem:

When performing comedy, I have a set routine. It's my comedic lesson plan. Some comedians never deviate from it. I may have performed my set hundreds of times and I know that my material works. Then I can be on stage one night and nothing seems to be going right. I should be getting laughs, but all I'm getting is all small tattering of laughter and smiles. I could say what many comics say: "It's a tough crowd." But I'm a professional, I do my set, and manage to do okay. Did I bring the house down? Maybe not. Did you bomb so badly that they will never have me back again? No, because I kept my composure and did not let the audience get to me.

So, what can be done? Since we know that no two snowflakes, comedy audiences, or classrooms are alike, it's imperative to individualize our presentation for each group. What goes well for one audience may not be the right cup of tea for the other. The comic has two instincts: Fight or Flight. One is to be angry, choose to bail on the audience, and start blaming them for not laughing and being a tight crowd. This will not win over any patrons, or club owners. The alternative is to dig in and use every resource to get that crowd laughing no matter what it takes.

Solve Comedy Problem:

One of the biggest lessons I ever learned in comedy was to be present in the moment. I let the audience know that I am there, and in the now. In a live comedic performance, I am following my outline, but I need to be ready at any moment to adjust to what is going on in my surroundings.

As a performer, I try not to let my material come off as too rehearsed. It has to have that "in the moment" feel. One essential skill of a comic is learning effective crowd work. An effective comic doesn't just step onstage and tell jokes. The effective comic scans the room, looking for audience reactions and details and issues so they can comment on it. If the room starts to feel like a funeral home, the smart comic will take advantage of that for material. The effective comic will scan the audience and look for additional inspiration. The comic will engage the audience with non-scripted moments of genuine interaction. Comedy is a two-way conversation.

One evening at a packed comedy club, the comics before me were all doing their standard material that would usually do well. For some reason, their jokes were flat and the crowd was very silent. I picked up this right away and knew that I not be doing my usual set. When I got on stage, I acknowledged the previous comics, making light of their weak sets. I made a point not to come off as mean. That would have just put me down the comedy hole even further than the other comics.

The key to having a good set for me that night was my ability to deviate from script and begin working the crowd. It was almost like I was my own opening act. As I probed the audience with background questions, I found out that most of the audience was not from the area and there were several pockets of tourists in attendance. Right away this locked into my brain. I realized that this was the only thing the crowd had in common in this unfamiliar comedy club. The audience was from all over the United States and even Europe. Just like a reporter, my fact finding mission began with questions like who, what, when, where, and why. I started to weave my material into my connection with the audience. Finally, I was able to bring them together as a group.

Living in Florida, I have played to many audiences of ages 65 and up. I know right away I'm going to do certain things: I keep any potential obscene language out of my act, I slow down my pace, I am more animated in the presentation of my material, and I try to be as likable as possible. Finally, I will acknowledge the fact to the audience that they are an older crowd. They buy into me because I am in the moment. I will not wait for that sinking feeling of *What's wrong with the crowd?*

As a comic, you have to know that every audience is unique. There are so many variables that can affect your show. It could be a work night. They could be drunk. They might be tired. They can be conservative. They can be young. As a comic, this is par for the course. You don't change your act; you just adjust to the moment.

Transfer to the Classroom:

Teaching middle school, I have learned that students' moods can swing at the drop of a hat. I love to state the obvious. So, when I see my classroom drifting off into Xbox heaven, I know to act fast. I love to gauge each class. If I find myself in the middle of a lesson and notice the engagement dwindling, I don't just keep going. I must stop acknowledge the situation. I tell them a quick story or make comments on the subject. It's like I have to kick start them back into focus. It's so easy to tell when I am losing my students. I just randomly ask a question about what we were doing five minutes ago. If I get a blank, I know that I have to "train my dragon" again if I want to get them engaged.

Classroom Example:

As a teacher, I know not every topic is going to be engaging with every student hanging on every word of the lesson. I do know when a topic is completely turning them off. I have learned through experience: I was teaching a lesson on "The Great Compromise" which deals with the conflict between the large states and the small states regarding representation in Congress. This is not the normal YouTube video that your students watch at night. It was clear that they were flat lining.

So, without hesitation, I told them to close their books and I proceeded to crumple up my lesson and throw it over my shoulder. I now had the students' attention on every word. I know that they rarely see teachers throw their lesson away. In their mind they are wondering: "What he is going to do next? Is he going to just give us free time and let us talk?" They wish.

Now I bring my stool out to the front of the class. Whenever I talk to students, or make comments on random items, or just want to see what going on, I always do it the same way. It is like Pavlov's dog. They know when I'm sitting on that stool closer to them, that I am in the moment.

Even though I know where the conversation is headed all along, it's still pseudo improvisation. You act as though there is a problem and you need their help fix it. Students love to give opinions and advice. This time it is solicited. I ask for feedback on the lesson and they will do their best to help me out. They feel as though you have allowed them into the inner sanctum of the education process and their point of view matters. Just a few minutes prior, they were in 'sleep mode', and now they are highly engaged. You now have the opportunity revise the lesson on the spot. You are in the moment. The students are impressed because they truly believe they have a hand in how they are being taught. This is something they rarely see, and to them, it's refreshing.

One thing I always have with my lesson is a "Plan B" just for situations like this. Does it involve a drastic deviation of the lesson plan? Of course not. I always try to have humorous hooks and previews such as *YouTube* or *Brainpop* video for each lesson. It just takes a few minutes of brainstorming but it's time well-invested. The students believe they are part of the creative process, and it gives them a sense of control and a close-knit classroom community.

Classroom Example:

So, how do I change lesson plans or deviate instruction? I have two ways to re-engage them. The first way is to involve the students directly. I will select one to two students to use as examples as my "learning puppets." I try to pick students who will play along and can be easily directed. So, back to my lesson on The Great Compromise: There are many real life examples of compromise that I can use metaphorically. There is always one side bigger than the other side. I can use the big kid and the littlest kid (without embarrassing them, of course) to make my point.

I ask the students to brainstorm examples of a school situation that would require a compromise. I could make it about food servings, locker usage or sporting activities. The kids play along at my direction. The class is engaged, and now I make the connection to the Great

Compromise while referencing to the two students for the rest of the lesson which gets a laugh. To think, 10 minutes ago, the class was lost on a flight to nowhere. Don't be afraid to deviate to the moment.

The second way is by using my SMART Board I know I can pull up any picture or any clip that will relate to the situation. Remember the attention span is shrinking all the time. So, if it's just a minute clip, it's fine.

Ultimately, I realized my mistakes were in the presentation. With a few STAND-UP strategies, I created a new and improved presentation that had the blessing of the classroom. Students believed I came up with it off the top of my head. That's what I wanted them to believe. They were now in the moment with me.

Review Steps:

1. Your brilliant lesson plan is sucking all the oxygen out of your classroom, like a scene from *Total Recall*.

2. Be in the moment. This can happen at any time during your lesson. If the lesson is not going well, you should acknowledge it. Your students will respond to the fact that you have showed them that you are not perfect and can mistakes like anyone else.

3. Take a quick, yet honest, reassessment of the temperature of the room. Try to have a backup plan. Make it seem spontaneous. It will earn the street cred with the students.

4. Make them part of the decision-making process.

5. Five minutes of research can save the whole day.

Reflection Questions:

1. Think of a time when one of your "best" lessons failed to engage all students?

2. What can you do to re-engage students who are not participating fully in your lessons?

3. How can involving students in the decision-making process in invigorate your classroom?

CHAPTER 9
"D:" DROP THE DEAD WEIGHT:
VAMPIRE TEACHERS

Problem in Classroom:

Have you ever talked to a teacher-friend who is a total downer? It's sunny outside, yet a rain cloud seems to follow them around. Because you are friends, they are always coming to you and complaining about everything. You do your best to help them solve problems because that is the way you are. You will not abandon your friend. But the problem is not just with you. You find out that they talk to every teacher in their sphere of influence, and tell them the exact same thing they were telling you. They pollute the mood of one teacher after another, and nothing can make them happy. Before you know it, your mood has been polluted, too. It's like some frowning alien has transplanted its negativity into your brain, or you have become the computer that has a virus trapped in its system. You did not start the morning planning on it, but now it's there. Now, in a bad mood, you have to get ready to start the school day.

The bell rings for the first class. The students were expecting Dr.

Jekyll, but instead got Mr. Hyde. The students are the ones that had to deal with the creature that you transformed into. You were hypersensitive and everything was setting you off in the classroom that normally would not have. That day you were the dictator of your classroom, and compromise was not in your vocabulary.

Students react to this sort of teacher behavior in two ways. First, they will be completely quiet, fearing you will write them up for the slightest infraction. Second, the student who loves to test your boundaries is going to attack the fence like an angry velociraptor. Normally, you have patience to solve any problem. However, since you're in a heightened state of agitation, if anyone tests your authority in the classroom, they'll get the wrath of your inner T-Rex. More than likely, there will be some verbal altercation, and administrative referrals will be written. Classes from each side of your hallway will also become quiet because everyone loves to hear when something's "goin' down" in another classroom. The news of your transformation will spread quickly around the campus, and students will tepidly come into each class. Why? It is because you let someone sap your teaching mojo.

Comedy Problem:

Stand-up comedy is such an ultra-competitive field. When comics are watching you, part of them actually wants you to do bad because it will make them look better.

Have you ever seen the ancient Greek symbol for comedy? It's the happy mask and the sad mask stuck together. Comedy is making laughter out of tragedy. Many comics fuel their act with all the baggage that they have been carrying over the years. To ask them how they are doing is to open a Pandora's Box of every type of mental neurosis. The negativity is like a tsunami washing away your happiness and leaving you stranded on an island of bitterness.

Bitterness is the word I would most associate with 80% of the comics I know. They are comics, but not "famous" comics. They are bitter about not getting on TV, about watching other comics getting breaks, about not getting bookings, and about having to play at venues they seem beneath them. "Why have I been forsaken?" is their mantra.

I've noticed that is the norm for about half of the comics hanging out at a club before a show. I go to a club with the intention of focusing on my set, but now I have to weave myself through a minefield of comedic psychosis. Chances are, they are going to want you to join them in their misery, because it really does love company. If I'm not careful, I will be dragged down to "Dante's Comedy Inferno," a place where bitter comics reflect on bygone eras, missed opportunities, and their jealousy of others.

If I let myself fall victim to this mind game, it will have negative effects on my performance. I might find myself apathetic about everything and just go through the motions of my act, while believing that the audience should be grateful for my appearance alone. They have no idea what is going on in my maligned and tortured soul. If there are any hecklers I would proceed to verbally obliterate them. If I let this happen, I will have lost my professional edge.

Solve Comedy Problem:

If you want to be a comic and have a lasting career you have to realize that having a good attitude is half the battle. There are hundreds of comics trying to work in clubs, and only so many opportunities. Club owners like to have comics that will keep the evening drama-free. The point is, you can easily be replaced by someone who they like. Comedy clubs enjoy a comic that is going to make the show run smoothly. Unless you are a really big act, clubs will not put up with a prima donna or a bitter attitude. The goal is always to keep working, and not jeopardize future opportunities. Having a family and being a teacher has really helped to get my priorities straight.

Time management is such an important part of everyone's life. With my hectic schedule, I finally realized that with comedy: I'm a professional and I'm here to do a job. I get to the show early and I ask to speak with the people in charge. I want them to feel comfortable that the show is all set to go. When I get to the club, I exchange pleasantries with the other comics, but I purposely keep my distance. On stage, my energy is such that I go a million miles an hour, but if you meet me before a show, you would never guess it. I'm usually sitting down looking over my notes in a corner. When comics come over, I try to steer the conversation to non-comic issues. I ask them about their families, and about the good things that are happening in their lives. I try to give off a vibe that I'm busy going over material. This keeps the pre-show conversation short and helps me maintain the right frame of mind: I'm there to do a show.

Many of the comics I know have their pre-show ritual commiserating in their bitterness and misery. Which is fine, because for some they are able to channel that and go on stage. For me, it's unproductive and I don't need the negativity. After the show, it is different, my job is done and I will engage the comics. Since my show is over, my attitude is different, and now all topics are open for discussion. I usually do not stay long after a show, but I do value taking time to converse with my comic brethren. Underneath it all, they are really funny guys and gals who are trying to deal with the pressure that comes with going "all in" on comedy. I can totally relate with it.

Before teaching, I was the same way, and sometimes I still get into a good industry-bashing session. Nobody is perfect. I know, for my own mental and professional health, it's important to keep things as stress free as possible. It's tough, but my show will be better in the end. Because I have been doing comedy for years, I have been able to develop wonderful, healthy relationships with comics who have become incredible friends. They are positive and upbeat. When

I see them at shows, the last thing we talk about is the business. We know we have a job to do. That comes first.

Transfer to the Classroom:

The teachers' lounge is like the green room of a comedy club where everyone is waiting to go on stage. In a room full of teachers, with the state of teaching in American today, what do you think they are going to talk about? I have to decide what I want to process and how to take control of the conversation. Are there issues that need to be discussed that get our blood to boil? Of course there are, but we can't put our collective heads in the sand.

Negative people have the potential to set a negative tone for my day, which is the last thing I need as a teacher. I'm aware that there are people who are always going to be the downer of the group, and in education, we all know that issues can sprout up at any time to take our focus away from being as professional as we can be.

When I get to school, I make sure to prioritize my preparation for that day. Only after I have taken care of my agenda will I pop in on my fellow teachers to see how they are doing. I always make sure to have a folder with me. This is just a passive way of conveying I have work to do, and don't have much time to chit chat. I always do my best to smile and be cordial. I explain what I have going on. I do acknowledge any conversation and will tell colleagues that I will need to get back to them during the day. The key is not to be rude about it and just blow someone off. That can lead to office gossip, and negative attitudes toward you. It's all about sincerity: a little kindness will go a long way. If you remind yourself of that every day, eventually it will become a habit.

Another key is not to lose focus on preparation and productivity. If I am prepared it will save me a lot of extra work at the end of the day and allow me to avoid bringing it home. Just like I schedule time in the day to get things done, I also make it a part of the day to go and check in with my colleagues. I devote part of my planning period every day to making my rounds of the campus, while completing administrative duties. I pop in on staff and administration; I will sometimes just do a quick peek into to a classroom of my friends. It's a quick interlude, a message to talk after school, or perhaps to call later on in the evening. It's only ten to fifteen seconds and I make sure not to interrupt direct instructional time. What could have taken up my morning prep time is now built into a friendly time management routine. I still have my friendship credibility and I have avoided the chance to be bogged down by serial talkers or complainers.

Classroom Example:

There are many teachers that are burnt out on the educational system, and can't acknowledge that they need professional help. They have given so much over the years and all of the stress of the education system has finally gotten to them. They have a broken and cantankerously negative attitude about education. Even when you attempt to put a positive spin on an educational topic or initiative, you are only met with a sneer. It has become clear that they are set in their ways, and can only make changes if they make that decision on their own.

You may feel guilty, because they are your friends and colleagues, but you can't continue to have your attitude polluted by this person's negativity every day. You have to decide how you are going to make that professional break without hurting them.

Distancing yourself from a friend and coworker is a delicate balance. You have to take charge of conversations. When they come into your classroom, you should talk to them, but continue to work. Explain that you have many things to do. The fact that the person saw you working conveys that you are not going to join their pity party. Do not make it a priority, because school work is the priority. When conversations come up and they get into their negative mood, interrupt and ask: "What's the solution?" You may find that they don't want solutions, but they just want to vent for the millionth time. Try your best to redirect them, and the key is not to be bullied into a negative conversation.

If you're firm and consistent in your behavior, eventually the person will realize that you will not be a part of their negative universe. It will take a while, but they will eventually find a new host for their parasitic behavior. The vampire will find a new neck to sink their negative teeth into. Now when you see the person, the conversation and tone is different. You've designed a new parameter for your friendship. You have taken charge as to what will influence your day at school.

Review Steps:

1. You have a coworker friend who is a toxic in their negativity, and is transferring it to you.
2. Acknowledge, that for your well-being, you have to finally do something about the situation.
3. Develop a plan that will not totally alienate the person, but alienate their negativity.
4. Take control of the conversations. Have the strength to interrupt.
5. Offer quick solutions to their problems. Do not let them get long-winded in their bouts of educational depression.
6. When you see the individual, you start the conversation. You keep it positive. If negativity creeps in, quickly switch the subject.
7. Use body language to convey that you are busy.
8. After a while they will start to leave you alone because their negativity bank is not being filled by you.
9. They will latch on to another teacher that feels the same way.
10. You have successfully changed the dynamics of your relationship based on positivity.

Reflection Questions:

1. How do you cultivate positive relationships with your colleagues?
2. Describe a situation where you have encountered negativity in the workplace. How did you deal with the situation?
3. What are some positive steps you can take to maintain friendships, but not fall victim to "Teacher Vampirism"?

CHAPTER 10
"U:" USE THE KITCHEN SINK

Classroom Problem:

Back when I was in school, and for many students today, the way of instruction was traditional and teacher directed. The teacher would stand at the front of the class and lecture. After the lecture there would be an assignment. It still works but it's not as effective as it once was. Today, student attention spans are shrinking by the minute. As a teacher, I have to be able to differentiate my instruction to get my curriculum to my students' brains. It can be a big challenge to find the right approach that my students will be receptive to.

Comedy Problem:

In comedy, a "monologist" is a comic who stands in front of the audience and either tells jokes or funny stories. It's known as "old-school comedy." The best examples of that would be Jerry Seinfeld, Bill Cosby, and Jay Leno. They have a point of view, and deliver their material to an eager, willing audience. Today, the eager willing audience is made up of millennials, the "instant-gratification" generation. It has to move fast. It has to be broken up. As a comic, I have to bring it to them, instead of the audience waiting patiently for a punchline. Many of the old school comics could never make it today. They would have a hard time developing. A starting (open mic) comic today only gets about three to five minutes. The comic must deal with distractions from cell phones, drunken hecklers, people ordering drinks, short attention spans, and an atmosphere where the attitude is one of less tolerance. Today, you have 60 seconds to be funny or it's "Bring on the next comic."

Solving the Comedy Problem:

In today's world, the breakout comics are those who have learned to play to multiple senses. Comedy is not from your forehead to your chin. It involves all your body. There is physicality to it. The masters are the late Robin Williams and Jim Carey. Today, look how many of the successful comics have used them as role models.

Many comics make a total performance out of their act. As a comic, you want to use expressions, gestures, postures, mimicry, choreography, and movement across the stage to make your point, you also must learn to emphasize details that give punch to your delivery. You want to play upon other senses, including the visual. At the same time, any story you tell should make an effort to appeal to as many of the five senses as possible.

Good jokes become better when they are acted out. The audience now sees and hears your vision of the world. This is called an "act out" which takes a joke from premise and punchline to a kind of sitcom-like scene where the observation is applied. It's a "show and tell" in reverse. You tell the joke and then show it. I have a joke with the premise of visiting Kentucky and finding out they had a "redneck vampire." I ask the audience: "How could you tell?" The punchline is: "He only has one fang." I then act out the premise with one hand flapping like a bat, and with my other hand at my mouth showing one finger coming out, representing the fang. I then use a slow, southern drawl to act out the character. He says he doesn't want to drink your blood, but instead, he'll take a bud light. I know, put me in the comedy hall of fame for such "brilliant highbrow material." The point is: it works. The bit has blended together the audio and the visual to cater to the multiple senses of the audience.

Transfer to the Classroom:

Howard Gardner (1983) pioneered the theory of multiple intelligences in his famous book *Frames of Mind*. He wrote about seven different ways people learn, based on their aptitudes for musical, verbal, logical, bodily-kinesthetic, interpersonal, intrapersonal, naturalistic, and existential aptitudes. With this knowledge, it's essential to include everyone in the lesson by playing to each student's particular intelligence(s). Just as a joke can seem narrow and one-dimensional if it's only a premise and a punch line, teaching can seem narrow and one-dimensional if it lacks sensory enrichment by only playing to a limited number of intelligences.

Playing upon multiple senses and acting out comedic material is similar to what effective teachers do when they broaden the material beyond words in a textbook and lecture. Effective teachers use visuals, sounds, tactile experiences, and the student's prior knowledge to engage them in a richer learning experience. They use PowerPoints, tell stories, use short video clips, computer resources, and music, and bring items and artifacts to enrich their student's experience. In short: we use everything, including "the kitchen sink."

Classroom Example:

As I approach lesson plans and learning goals, I always reflect upon how I can effectively convey the material while still being myself, having fun, and getting the students engaged. The first thing I do is to break the curriculum into manageable pieces, starting from the easiest material (basic knowledge and vocabulary), and then building upon that to reach the more conceptual material (analysis and synthesis in Bloom's Taxonomy) until students master the particular content. I know the students have limited attention spans. Instead of teaching for the whole period, and then asking if the students have questions, I break each lesson into brief, eight-to ten-minute segments. Each "mini-lesson" has a start, a middle, and an ending. Many times I use a countdown clock. I tell the students give me 10 minutes of their attention. The students understand this. They know I will not be rambling the whole period. After each segment, I give them a one to two minute break that is also on the countdown clock and then we start all over. During this time, I allow them to engage socially (because they need to, and have earned it). I can perform any administrative classroom tasks, and get myself ready for the next segment.

My personality dictates the way I teach. I am very animated and love to bounce around the class. The students can't help but notice me. I ask many rhetorical questions as a way of emphasizing key points for the teaching segment. By teaching in small chunks, I am able to maintain my energy level and keep my students engaged. Long gone are the days of handing students a worksheet and a book, and having them turn it in at the end of class. Today, I make every question a group learning opportunity or even a Socratic discussion, instead of subjecting students to the monotony of book work.

When it comes to delivering the content, I use The Comedy/Teaching Craft to play to the students' multiple intelligences. Within the first few weeks, students are aware that I love to go off on tangents, which could be telling a quick, funny story about the subject. I try to find the weird connections, because that's what kids find entertaining. One could compare this to a 20-30 second lead guitar riff in a song, after which I go back to the song, or in this case, the curriculum. I get the laugh and I'm out. I learned in comedy that you really can't milk a laugh that long.

Students are so visual. I will always cue up pictures of people, items, and events that will enhance the curriculum. Not only do the students see what they are learning about, they know that I'm inevitably going to make fun it. History has such an array of different characters, different fashions, and styles. When looking for visuals. I search for the ones that look the funniest in dress and appearance. I then make a comment on who it looks like in popular culture, and how it would apply today. It's a good laugh, it's memorable, and the students are learning.

What really gets the students laughing is to relate the reference to someone at the school. I will never pick on a student when saying what a picture reminds me of. That could get a laugh but it is just plain mean. On the other hand, members of the staff are fair game. At the beginning of the year, I ask some of my teacher-friends if there is any way (without being inappropriate or unprofessional) that I might just make a quick reference or impression of them (and by this I mean their "character"— see Chapter 11 for more on this!). If they're OK with it, I'm going to do it. The students laugh. Why? Because it usually something very noticeable, and I'm just validating that it is funny. It might be the way they talk, or a certain feature they have. It gets a laugh. I also do not shy away from making any self-deprecating remarks about myself if the moment is right. This shows the students that I'm human, and they appreciate it. It builds our classroom culture and helps with the learning process.

I am not a prop comic, but I am a prop comic teacher. If I'm ever out shopping and find something that would fit in with the classroom or enhance the subject matter I will buy it and use it in class. For example, I don't use pointers in my classroom, I use Star Wars light sabers that actually shoot out like in the movies. It's something different, and if I can use them to go off on a pop-culture tangent, I will. I have a whole box of toys that once belonged to my children that I will use in the classroom when the moment arises. It could be hand puppets, voice changers, or anything that has a sound effect. Students with auditory intelligence love sound effects. The key is to find the right balance between overusing the props and using them to enhance the learning in the classroom.

Sometimes lectures are inevitable, but I do my best to make them more engaging. If I'm talking about something mundane and I see an opportunity to use a funny voice or prop, I am going to do it. I often use the voices and movements of popular cartoon characters. The students enjoy it, they get to laugh, and sometimes they can do the impersonation better than me. I am all too happy to give them recognition and praise, and then it's always back to the learning. I have developed cues to get them back on task. I have a speaker button that plays Darth Vader's "Imperial March" theme music. My students know when they hear it, and see the "serious face" that accompanies it, then it's time to get back to work.

Review Steps:

1. Understand that individuals have multiple intelligences, or different ways they learn.
2. "Chunk" your lesson into segments of 8-10 minutes.
3. Use a countdown clock to display to the classroom, and have a one to two minute break between each segment.
4. Use your personality to be the driving force of your lesson plan.
5. Enhance your lesson with humorous tangents or visuals when possible.
6. Use appropriate humorous analogies revolving around school and staff.
7. Incorporate props and any hidden talents you have into your lesson.
8. When delivering curriculum, make your best effort to use physical movement and break up vocal patterns.

Reflection Questions:

1. How do you differentiate your instruction to a wide range of learners and account for each individual's learning style?
2. What aspects of your personality or "hidden talents" can you incorporate in your lessons to show students your humanity?
3. List five ways that you "use the kitchen sink" in your classroom.

CHAPTER 11
"P:" PHONY BALONEY

Classroom Problem:

Starting off the school year on a good note is paramount to your initial success. In the past, you may have noticed that the kids don't gravitate toward you or your lesson. They might think you're dull or boring. You have a love for your subject matter, but have trouble conveying it. You want your students to be as excited about the curriculum as you are. So, over the summer you read a couple of books, and you bought some props to use in the classroom. You can't wait for the new year to begin so that you can show your new students what a fun, cool teacher you are. You've spent time and money investing on this new persona that will make you the pied piper of your school. You're convinced this is going to be the best year ever!

The first day of school comes and you are ready to give your students the educational version of *The Full Monty*. You start your class with energy and exuberance only to be greeted with blank stairs and rolling eyes. You try again, and still not the positive response or appreciation you were expecting. Next period, you try again, believing the previous class failed to notice your genius. It gets the same response for every other class. Emotionally ravaged, you revert to the same teaching methods you've been using for years. Like every broken-hearted sports fan from Cleveland, you think: "There's always next year."

Comedy Problem:

Having good material is the quintessential key of being a good comic, but you have to deliver the goods. You have to find the right voice and character to give that knockout performance. You try imitating the style of your favorite comics, but it lacks credibility, and you will end up being called out on it. You try wearing different outfits on stage; you come up with a different voice and cadence to your delivery. It's failing, and it's because of YOU!

Solve the Comedy Problem:

You don't have to be Robin Williams, Jerry Seinfeld, or Ellen DeGeneres, they're a known quantity, and the world has seen them. If you want to be seen, get booked at clubs, and make it to television, you have to develop your own style. Every comic has comedy influences, but you have to know the difference between being influenced, and becoming a "persona thief." If you live and breathe a comic, you can do a tribute show to that person. I have seen comics do tribute shows to George Carlin and Sam Kinison. The show is advertised as a "tribute" because it's understood that it's not an original performance, but is an incredible impersonation of the celebrity comic's act. That is fine. The comic is not trying to pass off themselves as a comic legend, but are simply paying homage to them. Now, if they go up at a comedy club under their own name and start doing the act, it's a different story, and the comedy police will set the performer straight.

The biggest key is coming up with your own stage character. It can take years to develop, but once you have established it, it is like striking gold. The best comics are a caricature of themselves. This can be very difficult, because when you go on stage as yourself, you are bearing your soul to the audience. If you do well, it is fantastic for you. But if your act does not go over well, you see it as a condemnation of not only your act, but also of you. This can lead to overwhelming stress and fragile ego. Joan Rivers often talked about how when she started, she used her real name. When she bombed, it devastated her. When she changed her name to Rivers, she unlocked a new dynamic. Now if she bombed, the audience was not rejecting her, but were rejecting the character she created (1). If you can figure out how to separate the rejection of your character from personal rejection, you have conquered one of the biggest fears comics experience. You now have a foundation on which to build a solid act that is centered around a character based on you. A unique persona and perspective is what agents and club owners are looking for. You need something that makes you different from the rest of the comics, and that can be a career builder.

The way I developed my stage character was through feedback from comedic peers. When I first start doing comedy, I didn't pay attention to the inner workings of my character. My focus was on getting up on stage, doing my material, getting a great reception, and becoming more comfortable in front of audiences. For many people, public speaking is one of the most frightening activities on the planet. In addition, factor in the obligation to make people laugh after they've paid money for that experience. It is an incredible skill, and the great comics make it look easy.

After a year of doing amateur nights, I started to notice that many of my comic friends were starting to do imitations of me. At first, I thought they were making fun of me, and I resented it. I then realized that if they could imitate me, there must be something unique that I'm doing on stage. This was the foundation of my stage character. I started asking comics who imitated me: "Is this how I sound, and do I really act that way on stage?" They all said: "Yes."

So, I videotaped myself one night. After reviewing the tape, I noticed all the inflections and tones that I did on stage that the other comics were able to pick up on. What I realized was that the person on stage was "Mike Rivera" but with an exaggerated tone, speech delivery, and facial/physical gestures. I was then able to look objectively and realize that the character on stage, and the one that was being imitated was: "Mike Rivera to the second power." It was how I acted when I would get excited while watching a sporting event, or playing video games. It was not the Mike Rivera who was shy and socially awkward.

From watching the other comics, I was able to learn how to get into that character on stage and start to develop it. It was unique, and had many aspects of the outgoing person I always wanted to be, but was always too shy to be in social situations. On stage, and in character, I was now in a "safe zone." Whenever I found myself breaking character on stage, I would remember those comics who would do impersonations of me, and snap back to the level of energy and likability that continues to be the key to my comic success.

Transfer to the Classroom:

If there's one thing I've learned in my teaching career, it's that students can spot a phony. You don't have to be a Robin Williams (*Dead Poets Society*) or a Julia Roberts (*Mona Lisa Smile*) in the classroom. You can be, and have to be: YOU! Who knows yourself better? Kids have the most incredible intuition of being able to spot a phony, or someone who is putting on an act. The key is to embrace who you are, and make fun of it. Just as I did with my comic friends, ask your fellow teachers, friends, family, or students to do an impression of you. More than likely, they can. Watch that impression, take it, and run with it. You now have your core essence. You know what personality trait(s) you have to magnify. This is gold! You now have the ability to make a character of yourself. As long as you're thick-skinned, you can have fun with it. The students will enjoy your lessons more and it'll have a positive effect on learning gains. The breakthrough here is that you'll be able to have fun while teaching. It's infectious and will flow from you to the rest of the class.

It all relates to your likability factor. There is no law that says teachers have to be serious all the time. I remember the scene from *Ferris Bueller's Day Off* where Ben Stein is repeating: "Bueller...Bueller." Many times that is how your students see you.

Being likable to student's means having the qualities students can relate to and admire. Teachers must handle disruptions in the educational environment. Sometimes, teachers can jump in too early and lose their temper before anyone recognized that there was a problem. They could also be too late, allowing the disruptive behavior to continue for too long, and escalating a simple disruption to a crisis. Comics and teachers alike can "snap" in the face of a disruptive situation, and in their haste to shut it down they end up looking like a villain. If nobody heard little Johnny make a snarky remark, all they are going to notice is how mean the teacher was in putting Little Johnny in his place. Effective teachers don't rain blood and flames on students. They choose to be proactive to avoid the problem. If the problem comes looking for them, they frame the moment in which correction will take place. They use the right "touch" in terms of calling attention to the issue, and give the disruptive person an opportunity to stop. As a teacher, it may mean redirection or a friendly reminder: "Are you still will us, Suzie?" They are aware that there is a time to use the "big boy voice," but not in such a way that jeopardizes the relationship with the rest of the class.

Classroom Example:

I had a teacher friend who was having classroom management problems. At lunch, he would pick my brain and ask how I would handle certain citations. Before I knew it, students were telling me that the teacher was trying to copy my character and mannerisms. When I asked them if it worked, they said they could tell that he was a phony, and not himself. When I asked the teacher about it, he said he was still having problems.

So, as a favor, I made a list of his character traits that I had observed. He had a high pitched voice, with a Southern accent. He looked like Peter Griffin from *Family Guy*. He loved soccer and coached local teams. He had a very unique laugh. He never changed the tone in his speech. He loved westerns.

The next day, I went over the observations with him, and helped him write some comedic one-liners to use during class to relieve the tension and monotony. I told him he should use the "Peter Griffin" line first, because most of his kids knew *Family Guy*. He did, and got a big laugh from everyone. The key was for *him* to laugh about it. He was on his way to being likable, being himself, and most of all: not a phony. He continued with *Family Guy* references. He opened the student's eyes to soccer, all the things that it takes to make a great player, and all the places in the world he had played in. The students became more interested in him. He also allowed kids to impersonate his southern accent. They genuinely loved it (and he pretended to). Nobody likes to be the butt of a joke, but self-deprecation shows the students you are real. He was able to successfully magnify his observable character traits, and make light of them during his classes. He became less stressed. His classroom management was off the charts. He was able to apply the Comedy/Teaching Craft with his classes and was able to blend the academic and social side of teaching to great effect.

When I started my teaching career, I had the problem of wanting to be too likeable. This just led to being walked over by students. Give them an inch, and they'll take over the building. I learned I had to first establish my boundaries and have them know that the end game was about learning. Once that foundation was established, I found it a lot easier to be in control of the learning process and to be my likable self. Consistency was the key. I could now begin to implement my STAND-UP Strategies.

So, how did I keep it real with my students? It took a while. As a stand-up comic, I have to make off-the-cuff comments about everything. I started to do that in class and kept it school appropriate. If something good or bad was happening, they knew I would not sugar coat it. They respected that. I've done impressions and characters all my life, when the opportunity arises, I will use them. If I get a laugh, I will milk it for the entire day. If I'm doing an impression of Stewie from *Family Guy* and they like it, I will go to his voice for the entire lesson. Remember, at the beginning of the year I asked them about their favorite shows. If I can learn a voice, I do.

I learned what the students liked and what they didn't care for. Kids have incredible passions for things they like and especially things they don't like. So, if I find myself on the same side as them, they buy into the classroom dynamic more. For example, most students do not like standardized testing. I showed them the letter I wrote to the newspaper and school board. They respected it. They knew I was real, and they were ready to learn.

Review Steps:

1. Work on becoming a "character of yourself." This will make you funny.
2. You *are* funny. You have a sense of humor. You *are not* a robot. If something strikes you as funny, say it. Your students might not get it, but if you keep it up after a couple of weeks, they'll get you.
3. Make sure to laugh if you think something's funny. It will relieve tension and create a memorable moment.
4. Always do your research about hot topics and people that your students relate to.

Reflection Questions:

1. Have a friend or significant other write five physical traits and five character traits about you. You may not like them, but you have to realize that this is how the world is seeing you. Develop a "thick skin."
2. How can you magnify and exaggerate those traits to develop your character in the classroom?

   1. http://www.littlethings.com/shocking-joan-rivers/

CHAPTER 12

BONUS STRATEGY: PLAY TO YOUR ROOM, "THE CLASSROOM CASTLE"

A good Kung-Fu master always keeps some of the "secret techniques" hidden until the students are ready. This keeps the grasshoppers coming back for more. I will now honor you with one additional strategy.

Classroom Problem:

One of the first things I do when looking over any classroom is to see the room dynamics. Are you making the best use of your seating and class layout? Maybe you have bad Feng Shui.

Feng Shui:

1. *"The Chinese art of determining the most propitious design and placement of a grave, building, room, etc., so that the maximum harmony is achieved between the flow of chi (energy) of the environment and that of the user, believed to bring good fortune"* (or in this case higher test results) (Dictionary.com)

So, to clarify: the problem is your classroom, and you have to change the layout.

Comedy Problem:

In comedy, every room you play in has certain strengths and weaknesses. There may be a beam standing between you and the audience. This is common is barroom comedy where comedy was an afterthought when the club was built. The mic system may be weak, or the room may have horrible acoustics. Many clubs think all they need is just a mic stand and a speaker to have a show. To be honest, most one-night comedy gigs are like that.

You have to know the space you are playing in, and adapt to it. I recently played a club in Gulf Shores, Alabama where the audience was *50 feet* away from the stage. I guess the owner thought *intimacy* has nothing to do with comedy. In comedy: *intimacy is everything*.

There may be any number of distractions. These could include big screen TVs that are on during your set, the wait staff taking/serving orders from the bar or kitchen, or even a rock band playing in another room.

Solve Comedy Problem:

In comedy, I have to work with whatever stage setup is given to me. I have no idea until I get there. I have to analyze the room quickly to see where I will be most effective. I might have to stand on a different part of the stage. Sometimes they will have lighting that is misdirected and not hitting the stage square, so I have to make sure I am in sync with the lighting. If I want to do well, it is up to me to change position and bring myself to the audience.

If the audience is far away, I will move the mic stand to be closer. Yes, I could do my show from 50 feet away, and mail it in, but that's not up to my standards. People are paying good money to see me, and to be entertained. I have to make that connection. Sometimes, when the audience is far away, I will drop the mic and actually walk out into the crowd. This is a great technique because the audience believes it's an extemporaneous moment, and that I seem to have a reckless abandon, but in reality I planned it all along. I knew since I arrived at the club that this is what was it going to take to win them over.

Transfer to the Classroom:

Like bridging the gap in comedy, effective teachers must also take steps to manage their classroom space. In the classroom, one must take into account room size, windows, blind spots, and desk arrangement, etc. The goal is to manage the room maximize instructional potential.

The difference between comedy and teaching in this situation is that teachers are in a better position to physically alter the room. Teachers, in most cases, can create their own stage. They can move desks around to heighten visibility, and can customize their classroom layout to fit their needs.

Many teachers are afraid of changing their layouts out of fear. They are so used to having their students in rows. The teacher has built their own comfort zone, or *"Fortress of Fear"* within the classroom. Like most people, they fear change in their routines. They might feel comfortable, but it's it not what's best for the students. A teacher that can let go of fear and try something new has an opportunity to improve and increase effectiveness.

Bridging the gap means managing space in the classroom before the students come in. Consider the desired focal points in the room, and sit in the desks before school to get an idea of how you are going to be seen. Remember: desks are not barriers, they're desks! Don't use desks as a "Great Wall" or barrier to instruction. Tear down that wall!

Classroom Example:

When I decorate my room, I try to make it an extension of my own personality. Yes, I have sections designed for charts that convey academic necessities such as standards, learning goals, and achievement data. I decorate charts with pictures or quotes to draw attention to them during the school year.

I keep this section separate from the rest of my room, which I use to enshrine the gifts that students have made or given to me over the years. For example: I have fifty different *SpongeBob* toys from stores and Happy Meals. I have stuffed animal characters from *Family Guy* and *South Park*, which the students always enjoy. I also have a section of my wall dedicated to Chuck E. Cheese pictures of my kids and myself. I've had the privilege of taking many trips abroad, including to five of the seven continents. I have poster-size pictures of myself next to famous monuments in China, Costa Rica, France, Germany, Italy, Peru, and Spain.

I used to be one of those teachers who kept their students in traditional rows. It was a comfort for me. Rows can work well at the beginning of the year, when I'm setting class boundaries and learning students' names and characteristics. It was easy (and still is) to send any students with potential/chronic behavior problems to one of the four corners of "Dante's Classroom."

After a while, I noticed that certain students had difficulty learning from certain parts of the room. I always have a table in the front of my room for students who need to move up to see. I recommend this for teachers who want to wean themselves from the traditional row set-up. I also use this table to provide hard-copies of my classroom materials for those students who visual difficulties.

From visiting classrooms around the school, I have learned ways of manipulating seating charts to enhance learning and bring the class closer. Don't be afraid to visit the classrooms of your colleagues for ideas that work. Don't be afraid to try them, because you can always move them if it fails. I finally settled on blocks of four desks, with two students on each side, facing one another. I am careful to make my groups heterogeneous when it comes to ability levels. I never place all of the "A" students together, nor will I place all of the "D" students together. I try to facilitate peer support, and with that comes peer accountability. If I become aware that a certain group setup is going to be problematic, I may move them closer to me, but I don't automatically disband the group. Just as in the real world, students must learn to get along with, and work with others. Overall, this departure from traditional rows has encouraged my students to take a more active role in the learning process, in addition to the academic and social gains that come from collaboration.

Review Steps:

1. Analyze the layout of your classroom.
2. Sit in different seats and notice if there are any dead spots where delivery of curriculum could be enhanced.
3. Take a look at other layouts of classrooms in your school. You can also Google examples.
4. Don't be afraid to make radical shifts in classroom layouts. The students have no idea. They may believe you do this all the time.
5. You might have to totally change the direction of your room.
6. Strategically decorate certain areas of your classroom and maintain a theme to avoid confusion. Do not mix *SpongeBob* toys with rubrics.
7. Make sure desks are not barriers. Convey openness.
8. Teach to the strength of your classroom layout.

Reflection Questions:

1. Give some examples of how your classroom reflects your personality.
2. Consider your seating chart: Is it a product of teacher comfort or an avenue for student success?
3. Compare your classroom to a peer's classroom that has a different layout. Discuss the strengths and weaknesses of each layout.

PART IV
Real Life Issues and Inspirations

CHAPTER 13
THE STAND-UP TEACHER'S GUIDE TO: HECKLERS

A heckler is a person who harasses and tries to annoy others with questions, challenges, or personal attacks. Hecklers are often known to shout disparaging comments at performers with the intent of disrupting performers and/or participants. At a comedy club, hecklers are an uninvited pest to your performance. There is no lower form of life on the planet. In the classroom, hecklers are often a part of your classroom dynamic. For your students and your sanity, it is important to address them immediately.

Comedy/Classroom Problem:
A Guide to Identifying the Types of Hecker

The Troublemaker:
We humans love to slow down and watch the aftermath of a car accident or see a disaster film. Some humans enjoy creating trouble, and like The Joker, "want to watch the world burn."

The Troublemaker (Student Version):
Some students just want to create chaos in the classroom. They

know which teachers have a reputation of losing their composure at the drop of the hat. The other students are sometimes tuned into what will happen. To the Troublemaker, peer attention is a merit badge.

*The Troublemaker

Apathy Incarnate:

Perhaps they were dragged to the club to cheer them up after something miserable has happened in their life. In comedy, these are the people in the front row with their phones out, busily texting. It's like playing to a statue that is three feet away from you. They try their best to "stone face" you, and, like a comedic gladiator, challenge you to make them laugh.

Apathy Incarnate: (Student Version):

Most teachers go out of their way to make lesson plans engaging and entertaining. The non-participant student has already determined they are mentally vacant when it comes to your class. You can be talking right to them, but they are a million miles away. When you ask them a question, it's like talking to a brick wall. Their favorite lines are: "I don't know," and: "Can you repeat the question?"

Apathy Incarnate

The Know-It-All:

Did you mispronounce a word, forget the year a movie came out, or make even the slightest stumble on stage? This jerk is there to point the finger, and make it known to the audience that he or she is clearly superior.

The Know-It-All (Student Version):

This is the student who has been micro managed by his parents since conception. The student patiently waits for the teacher to make the slightest error, and then, like a lion pouncing on the gazelle, they make their move to show how vulnerable you are. They claim victory, and unfortunately have to go back to their structured life-pods they call home. It's the only fun they will have during the school year.

The Know-It-All

The Attention Seeker:

"Hey honey, watch this," is usually the first thing out of their mouths. They've likely watched a few too many stand-up specials, and can't wait to throw you one of their favorite one-liners. It makes for an awkward moment when the audience realizes that this person isn't drunk; he's just unaware of what a jackass he is.

The Attention Seeker (Student Version):

You're halfway into your lesson, you have given instructions and reviewed all viable information. Every student is on task, and then you hear: "I don't get it!" At first, you're taken off guard. How could anyone not get this basic concept that I have spoon-fed to my students? You ask probing follow-up questions, only to realize the student really doesn't get it. They aren't faking their lack of knowledge but they are demonstrating their lack of motivation and effort. They are the students who have learned to be helpless. They have problems in every class. They have fallen through the cracks of the educational system. They have never been taught manners, and see absolutely nothing wrong with interrupting on a whim.

*The Attention Seeker

The Drunk:

A lot of clubs have a two-drink minimum, but few have a maximum. Many of these tortured souls come to the comedy club to escape from a long week, but often they will be loud and obnoxious. They will embarrass themselves, their friends, and anyone who is unlucky enough to be their companion. Often times, they have to be escorted out. It can get ugly. They will not remember it in the morning, but the comic and the audience will.

The Drunk (Student Version):

Just remove the word "drunk" and replace it with *angry/inconsiderate*. They are in need of an adult who will take an interest in them or set them in the right direction. This is where mentors and life coaches are needed in the educational system.

Comedy/Classroom Solution:

The key to handling most hecklers is not to take their behavior personally. You need to separate yourself from the problem in order to deal with it. If you take it personally, you just make the problem worse by feeding into the tension, and giving the heckler power. That detachment might be hard to achieve, but it is essential if you want to deal with the problem and recover. In comedy, the comic has the microphone, and can drown out the problem by talking over it. In the classroom, a teacher cannot. They must actually deal with the problem. Everything is heard, and is "on the record." Try the following methods when faced with these situations:

1. Ignore the problem.

Give a verbal cue (perhaps one that you have established during the first few days of school) that shows your dissatisfaction and hope the problem with correct itself. This takes the least amount of energy, and only works with classes that have really bought in to your system. However, if it's the beginning of the year or if you're trapped in a den of wolves, the group is expecting you to become *the pack leader*.

2. Let the audience/class help you.

Chances are, they will be on your side if someone is being rude to you. The group will often provide backup by expressing dissatisfaction with the heckler. You can encourage this by directing your responses to the group, and not the heckler who is craving the attention. Never challenge the heckler to a battle of wits. This would be focusing your attention on one person, and leaving out the rest of the group. Things will just escalate and make everyone uncomfortable. You run the risk of losing the whole group. Try to make this a teachable moment.

To do this, you must isolate the inappropriate behavior, and you make the heckler look foolish without directly challenging them. Furthermore, you start to build an alliance with the group that heckling behaviors are not accepted in the classroom. If you can reframe the situation as: "us against the heckler," then the group will be on your side no matter what happens. Remember, make your response a reaction to the inappropriate behavior and do not make it a personal attack on the individual.

3. Use the problem to advance your character.

A lot of comedians will break character or resort to a stock heckler response or just lose their cool. If you do this, you are wasting a valuable opportunity to advance your persona. You can turn this negative into a positive by showing the group how "you" (but really your character) would deal with the problem. This will come off as an honest response and will give the group a deeper glimpse into your personality. In a sense, it will prove to them that you are: "who you say you are," thus building credibility. If your style is quiet and low key, and you respond the same way, your response will be real. If you respond harshly, the illusion you created with your character will be shattered. The heckler has won because you have lost control.

This is an advanced skill that has taken me years (under *the cruel tutelage of Pai Mei*) to perfect in the classroom. I know that I am being tested by the student's behavior. I always keep in mind that heckling is inevitable, but I am prepared for it. When an incident happens, I can remain in my character and keep my composure. I win, and the class wins. The heckler loses because my response has caught them off guard. It was not the response they were expecting.

4. Don't respond at all if you are not completely sure what the heckler said.

Once during a lesson, I heard talking in the back of the room. This was during a more structured segment that required quiet concentration. Having gone over the rules, I was surprised and even a bit disappointed to hear a clear violation of the instructions. The student meekly responded that she was just helping the other student find the correct page. The other student was shy, and didn't want to ask me. All I did was reinforce that student's shy behavior. I offered my sincere apology, because in that case, I messed up, and was unnecessarily harsh. In comedy, I could just keep going, but in the classroom, this situation was cause for a sincere apology. It's important to apologize to the class when you mess up in front of them. It shows humanity and models correct behavior that you would expect anyone else to do. Again, it adds to your credibility.

5. Pick Your Battles.

A lot of time, the group doesn't notice there's a problem until you draw attention to it. If a small group is talking, for example, see if it works itself out with just a quick visual que, and wait a few seconds before you say something about it. Only say something if you get the sense that the group is distracted too. The key is not to come across as an insecure control freak who will lose their head at the slightest of infractions. Keep your cool. Your students are always watching.

6. If the heckler says something that is funny (but not vulgar), acknowledge it!

It makes him feel like a hero, and makes you look like a nice guy (a teacher with a sense a humor), by giving the heckler some positive attention. In doing so, you might turn a potential chronic distractor into a valuable ally. Once during class, I was talking about the stock market. I was telling the class how the key to analyzing stocks was to buy low and then sell high to maximize the profit. A student in the back says sarcastically: "So, you sell your stocks when you're high!?" the whole class laughed, and so did I.

I quickly realized that I had left the student a comedic opportunity. He was paying attention, was able to think fast, and capitalized on it. Why not reward him? I allowed the student to a trip to my treasure chest full of "healthy snacks" to take one. By the way, Snickers, Kit Kats, and Skittles are "healthy." He later confided: "Normally, I would be yelled at by any other teacher." I told him that it was funny, and I chose to keep a positive attitude about it. A student that was usually a behavior problem now feels part of the class.

Review Steps:

1. With class disruptions, it's not a matter of if, it's a matter of when. Be prepared.
2. You have to be quick to keep your cool. The first thing you can do is smile to help diffuse the situation.
3. Do not to blurt out the first thing that comes into your head.
4. This is a difficult skill that takes practice and experience. Use the beginning of class as practice, especially when you have multiple students asking you questions rapidly. Practice giving quick, calm responses. Use that as your practice time. It will be time well-invested.

Reflection Questions

1. What is your plan for dealing with student disruptions?
2. How do you reward and encourage positive student behavior?

CHAPTER 14
A PICTURE IS WORTH A THOUSAND WORDS

I love this picture of my 8th graders (*as featured on my school's Facebook Page*). One of our teachers was being recognized by the Tampa Bay Lightning. Their marketing team was coming in to make a short clip that would be shown on the big screen at the arena during breaks in the action, or between periods. I always keep my door open for most of my day, unless the class is working on a group project that will get loud.

It was first period, and the students were still waking up as we worked on review questions about the American Revolution.

All of a sudden, I heard a bit of a commotion, saw a bunch of suits with camera crew coming down the hallway along with the Lightning mascot: *ThunderBug*!

I had to think fast. I deftly sidestepped into the hall, pointed at *ThunderBug*, and screamed:

"You! In my classroom! Now!"

The Mascot actually followed along! I whipped out my cell phone and set it to selfie mode. Then I thought: "Why not get the students in the shot?" So, I tossed my camera to the marketing rep and said: "Student picture time!"

I've never seen 8th graders move as fast as they did. She took two pictures, and all it took was two minutes. The kids were happy and excited to get back to work, but they did make fun of me for "hijacking" the mascot. During my planning period, I showed the pictures to my administrators and fellow staff members. It was put up on our school's Facebook page. The kids were really thrilled. They thought it was cool. That night, I made a personal copy for every student that was in the picture. The next day I passed them out, and the majority of them asked for tape so that they could put it on their binders. They were so proud of the picture and wanted it to be displayed for all their friends to see it.

The Point:

I received so many complements on the photo, commenting on what a great class I had. Many teachers thought they were advanced, but it was quite the opposite. A number of these students struggled with school. Most had to take multiple remedial reading and math classes. Suffice to say, there weren't too many bright spots in the day for these kids. Some students pointed out that for certain classmates, it was the first time they'd ever seen them smile.

At first, I was taken aback by this, but after 15 years of teaching, I get it. These are still children and not testing robots. They are all different and go through things in life we rarely get a glimpse of. So, if they have a hyper teacher who isn't afraid to drag a mascot into the classroom for two minutes, it just might make their day. A two-minute break, and picture with *ThunderBug* was all it took. It's all about the little things. These are the things that are never measured or evaluated by today's academic standards, but they're just as important.

CHAPTER 15
LESSONS FROM RALPH

Ralph Rivera was my father. He worked for Union Carbide from ages 18-55. He started out sorting the mail, and ended up having people with doctorates working for him. He had an incredible work ethic. He had an innate sense of wisdom and sensitivity. As a child, he suffered from injury that left his leg in a cast for two years. It caused his leg to suffer from atrophy, which made it smaller than the other leg. That experience provided him with an empathy for anyone who suffered from any type of handicap. He created employee programs to help paraplegic and quadriplegic workers. This was before the Americans with Disabilities Act. He would always say how smart they were and related that they could still use their hands, or even their mouths to manipulate computer applications.

"So, what does a wheelchair have to do with stopping them from doing a good job?" he would say.

Ralph also taught me to champion anyone who was "an underdog." He was a staunch believer in civil rights for all. He would advocate for all minority groups. As kids, we were unaware of his impact, because to our family, it was just normal to accept people for who they were, and not the color of their skin or sexual orientation. He was a cool dude, and a generation of ahead of his time. I am proud to be his son.

He always had a few little sayings that he would teach me. I have kept them throughout the years. I use them with my own kids and when applicable, with my students.

"It doesn't take that much to make someone happy."

"It doesn't take that much to make someone happy" was his favorite line. He knew that life was about the little things. Sometimes, we have no idea what a small random act of kindness means to anyone and more so a student. The littlest of niceties can mean the world to a student. It could be a few kind words as they enter the classroom, giving them a pencil, or just saying "hi" as they pass by in the hallway. Students remember that. It fills up your account in their street cred bank.

"Pick your battles."

How many times has a student shown up to class being unprepared without a paper or pencil? I have a supply box by my desk filled with pencils and paper. The students know they are always welcome to take what they need anytime. I choose not to berate them. Unfortunately, there are some teachers that still do. They will write them up for being unprepared and cause an unnecessary scene. Is this really something you want to go to war with a student over? Many times if I'm running low on supplies I will ask the class if they can loan something to another student until the end of class. This minimizes interruptions and potentially helps students make new friends.

"We are not mind readers."

Just because we live our lives in a certain way, we can't expect others to live the same way. We have no idea what is going on in the home lives of students. What might be a simple supply list to us, can be a major obstacle for families in need. I require a simple spiral notebook in my class for notes. Some students will not be able to get notebooks. When I go shopping I always see bargains for them. I always pick up an extra dozen. After a week or two, I will just walk by the student without one and just drop it off on their desk. The look on their faces is pleasantly shocking. They wonder: "why should the teacher go out of their way to help me?" It's just another way of building those classroom relationships that will make my year go smoothly and show students that I care.

I had a wonderful student, we'll call him "Maurice." The teaching staff knew his mom was moving him from shelter to shelter. He was bright and popular, and it was amazing to see how he kept himself motivated. After class, about a month into the school year, Maurice asked if he could talk to me. He wanted to know if I meant what I said when I told the class: "If they ever needed anything for school, just ask." He told me about his situation, and that he really needed the supplies for his other classes. I took Maurice to my supply closet and told him to grab everything he needed. He was so relieved. Throughout the year, my colleagues and I were able to get Maurice and his family connected to the right agencies for assistance. The wonderful volunteers were able to make sure that he and his family were being fed, and even had clothing they could be proud of. Maurice made honor roll every marking period and was accepted into a high school program that he was interested in. A couple of years later he spent his volunteer hours for high school as an assistant for me.

Maurice's story emphasizes how important it is to advocate for students and train them to advocate for themselves. It can often be difficult, and embarrassing, for individuals to admit that they are struggling. By building a safe environment that encourages openness, I was able to help Maurice meet his basic needs and overcome minor obstacles that could have been major barriers to his success.

"Admit when you are wrong."

Ralph would always tell me that "if someone thought they never make mistakes, then they are making mistakes." This means they are too myopic and narcissistic to think that they are infallible. "How can anyone be right all the time?" Today's students are skeptical and are aware of it. We live in a world where our heroes are constantly falling from their ivory towers, only to show a capacity to bounce back. We are a very forgiving society.

Back when I was in school, (I'm sounding older all the time), I believed whatever the teacher said was true. We believed the word of the teacher was coming from a higher power. They were to always be trusted and never, I mean never, questioned. Today, a teacher with that attitude would be done faster than you can say: "Common Core." Kids are subjected to so much in their lives. Due to this fact, many students come to school with a cynical, jaded attitude toward teachers, and adults, in general.

We are not perfect. We should not act that way. We do make mistakes, and when we can point it out to students it lets them know that we are "real." Students who are afraid of making mistakes will be encouraged by this practice, because it models that it is okay to be imperfect. Too much pressure is put on our students to come up with the correct answer. Just like adults, kids must learn from their mistakes. That's a great place to begin in your classroom. The result is: you have broken down another barrier to building a cohesive classroom community. That's all we can really ask of our students: "Show me effort!" Acknowledging efforts can win the students over.

I would not be a good (fill in the blank) if?

This was my father's all-encompassing catch phrase that could never be challenged. You can fill the blank with just about anything and your reasoning is set in stone. When I was kid, I would ask my dad:

"Could I stay out late?"
"Could I get a new guitar?"
"Can I go over my friend's house?"

He would answer: "Sure, I would like to, but then I wouldn't be a good parent!" *Bam!* I'm stuck in my tracks. What am I going to say? "I want you to be a bad parent." It doesn't fly.

I use this all the time in the classroom when students ask me why we have to do certain assignments. I tell them: "I would not be a good teacher if I did that." The line has proven to be indefensible in the classroom. By not wavering from the task, I am modeling responsibility. Just like there are repercussions for students who fail to do their work, they realize that it is the same for teachers. In a small way, you have now become "simpatico" with students. Steadfastness build your credibility, capitulation destroys it.

"Life is what you make of it in the present moment."

Ralph would always tell me that: "I can't do anything about the past or anything about the future." He would tell me that what I did have control of was: "what I was doing at this very moment." It was my choice, and any benefit or consequence can be traced back to that. Students are kids that for the most part, have short memories. How many times did your parents reprimand you, and the next day everything is cool. It's the same way with students. "Once it's over, it is over, and it's time to start again." I stress this with my students every day. I tell them: "Today is your new chance at life. It begins right now. I don't have the power. You do." This teaches the student to take ownership for their actions. It goes back to the choices and consequences paradigm.

Hope is such a powerful tool in the classroom. One of my rituals that I start at the beginning of the school year is to recite the message of hope from *The Shawshank Redemption*. "Hope is a good thing, maybe the best of all things, and good things never die." Within 10 weeks, my students will recite it with me before every test or standard exam. It works... I hope.

"You are not God."

Nobody is perfect. You will have failure. Nobody wins all the time.

You might go through a whole year and only remember the few kids that you could not reach. You can't dwell on it, or it will haunt you. All you can do is your best.

I had one student who, despite my best efforts, I failed to reach. I asked for help from just about the whole staff. I used all of my tried and true strategies. I had to learn to let it go. It's tough to take defeat. Investing time in students usually does pay off. When it doesn't, it's like a shot to the gut. The sooner I realized that I couldn't win every battle, the more students I was able to help.

My father would always ask me: "Did you try your best?" It could be from losing a little league game to a failure at a marriage. If I said no, then he'd say: "Well, next time, give it your best." If I said yes, he'd ask: "What more can you do?" It's time to let it go. There will be another opportunity.

CHAPTER 16
AMERICA'S MOST HILARIOUS TEACHER

"And the winner is Mike Rivera!" With those words from Sherri Shepherd, co-host from *The View*, I had won "America's Most Hilarious Teacher." It was a wild ride for three months leading up to that moment.

In early January 2013, I had come home late after a stand-up comedy show in Orlando. Before I went to bed I checked my emails. A friend had sent a quick note to say that the TV show *The View* would be accepting applications for a contest they were running to find "America's Most Hilarious Teacher." The contest would be judged on the teacher's ability to perform stand-up comedy. Since I have been doing stand-up comedy for years, I thought I should give it a shot.

I have never been a big fan of "the comedy contest." Many times the funniest person doesn't win, and sometimes you already know the winner before the contest started. But this time, something inside of me said: "go for it." So, I proceeded to *The View*'s website, filled out the online forms, and uploaded a suitable video clip of my stand–up routine.

About two months had passed with no response, I had relegated myself to believing that I had been passed over. That was about to change.

On February 20th, I was checking my email and saw a title that said: *"ABC Television The View: America's Most Hilarious Teacher."* The email said I was being considered for the show, and asked me to call the segment producers as soon as possible.

I gave a call to the producers, Jonathan and Vinny, who wanted to pre-interview me over the phone. They said my tape was very funny, and they had many people on their list they were considering. They asked me many background questions, and were very pleasant to me. Finally, they asked if I would be able to fly up to New York the following week. "Of course," I said. I would not pass up the opportunity. They also let me know that since there were so many potential contestants, that I really shouldn't get my hopes up... but I did.

The next day, I officially got the offer from ABC to do the competition to find "America's Most Hilarious Teacher." The competition format was to have one teacher perform a three-minute act each day of the week, in front of a live audience and three judges, then they would announce the winner the following Monday. I would be performing on Friday's show that would be taped on Thursday. This gave me the advantage of watching all of the others go before me. I was given numbers and names to call from the travel coordinators at ABC to set up my limo and hotel in New York City.

I was completely excited. I called my comedy friends over to my house to select the material that would pack the most "bang" for the short time I was to be on stage. I had to keep in mind that I would be performing to a studio audience of about 250 women. I came up with about five minutes' worth that I could edit during the week.

Pre-Show:
The next day, I was contacted by the local newspaper and three local

television stations that wanted to come and interview me during the school day. They would be interviewing my students and I, and filming me while I was teaching. My students were all excited for the opportunity to get on television. After busy days at school that week, I spent the nights at local comedy clubs practicing my set to work out the timing.

I flew up to New York the following Wednesday. I was picked up by limo and was put up in a beautiful hotel near Times Square overlooking the theater where *The Book of Mormon* was playing. It was tough for me to calm down. I called all my friends to get any anxiety I had out. I walked around the Theater District to focus my mind. It was beautiful.

I was to be picked up the next morning at 9:00 to get to ABC Studios. It was enormous. It took up an entire city block and had too many floors to count. I gave my name at the security gate and I was escorted to my dressing room. As soon as I got to room, Sherri Shepherd came and introduced herself immediately. She spent about 10 minutes making small talk with me. She could not have been nicer.

Since it was a Thursday, they were shooting two shows, so they could have Friday off. I would be doing the second show of the day. In the main waiting area, I met the segment producers Jonathan and Vinnie. I rehearsed my set for about 20 minutes with them. They wanted every word to be on target. All I had to do now was wait.

The other teacher comic had now arrived in the studio. She was a bit pompous and would tell anyone within earshot how funny she was. I kept my mouth shut and watched the first show from the green room. Since her set was live, a fellow teacher back home at my school had her class watch the segment. After her set, I was able to get a joke by joke review from one of her gifted students. His insights were brilliant and this really put me at ease. After her set, she came back to the common dressing room and was telling everyone how she had killed it, and asking when she would be called back as the winner. I just sat there and wished her well.

The second show would be taped an hour later. I'd be in the last segment, and it seemed like forever before then. With 15 minutes remaining before my segment, the producers came and escorted me to the soundstage. I was trying to keep focused but nerves started to creep in. I was in the green room that was next to the studio. Most of the guests of *The View* were there. I tried to remain calm and act as though I belonged. I was bumped into by Sigourney Weaver. She excused herself and introduced herself along with David Hyde Pierce, who she was working with on Broadway. They started making small talk with me. All I could think about was how cool this was.

The second to the last segment was about to start, and the floor producer took me to the set and showed me my mark on stage. The make-up artist did a quick touch up on me and I was ready to go.

"Kill This!"

Those were the last words of the floor manager as she opened the door. I walked out into the lights, and I proceeded to do my stand-up in front of the live studio audience. I remembered to smile and to be confident. The judges were Sherri Shepherd, Joy Behar, and Mario Cantone. During my set, I knew I was doing well. As I moved into my last bit, I decided to end my set at the apex of the biggest laughter. It worked. The audience gave me such a wonderful ovation. I could not have been happier. The judges all remarked favorably on my set. I could not wait until all my friends would see it the next day.

"Well you won!" were the words of the segment producers Jonathan and Vinnie after I was back in my dressing room. After my set, and seeing how the other comics were judged. I had a good idea that things were going to go well. They told me that I could not tell anyone, and I would be flying back to New York on Sunday night to be announced as the winner live on Monday's show.

It was tough to keep a secret with so many of my close friends and family. When I arrived at the studio on Monday, the whole studio was abuzz. Barbara Walters was returning that day after an extended absence and it was the biggest story in all of New York. The studio was filled with many well-wishers and celebrity guests. Regis Philbin, and Mayor Michael Bloomberg dropped in. I was told they had to cut time from my segment, which would be at the end of the show. The moment finally arrived: Sherri Shepherd announced me as "America's Most Hilarious Teacher." During my segment, they only had time to ask me three questions. I wasn't as nervous as before. When we went to a commercial break, Sherri said that she was so glad that I had won.

At the end of the show, I was informed that I would be flying back on that Thursday to film my own segment. I would be interviewed by Joy Behar in her *Comedy Corner* segment. No longer would I be considered a "contestant" or a "contest winner." I would be brought out as: "Mike Rivera, America's Most Hilarious School Teacher."

My "Celebrity" Debut

I arrived at the studio at 9:30 to rehearse my interview with the producers. The only other people in the studio were the stage crew. They were laughing during my rehearsal. That was a good sign. Because they were filming two shows on Thursday, I would have to wait almost four hours before I went on. This time I didn't have to hang out by myself. I had made friends with the crew. They basically adopted me. They knew that I was a teacher, and to them that made me a regular guy to them and not some "big time star with an attitude." I spent the rest of my time eating and hearing wonderful behind the scenes stories. They also took pictures with me and gave me mementos from my time on the show.

As the time approached for my segment, I was well prepared. I must have gone over the set a dozen times in my head. I reminded myself to enjoy the moment and to soak everything in. I will never forget hearing them call my name, walking to the middle of the stage, and looking at the cheering people. The feeling was incredible and surreal for this middle school teacher. The audience was great. I received over 12 applause breaks (not that I counted...) in my five minutes. After my set, the producers were patting me on the back, and the stage crew came over to congratulate me. As I was leaving the studio, the stage crew told me to wait up. As they guided me out of the studio, each of them wanted to tell me about a funny teacher they once had. It was a great way to end the trip.

I didn't return home till about 3:00 am. I had to call in for a substitute for the next day. I did, however, show up at school. The reason was so that I could take my son out of class and into an office and have him watch the segment with me. I will never forget how, as he was watching me on the television, he would turn his head every 20 seconds to look back at me. I guess seeing his dad on TV and having me right next to him was surreal for him too. When the segment was done, he gave me a big hug and told me that he loved me. It really doesn't take that much to make someone happy!

* Mike Rivera and cast of The View.

*Mike Rivera and Terry Crews.

*Mike Rivera and Whoopi Goldberg.

* At the table on The View.

CHAPTER 17
WHY DO I TEACH?

"Why do I still teach?" That is the $44,000 (a year) question! Over the past few decades, more and more teachers are leaving the profession. Pacing guides, standardized testing, being asked to do more with less every year, and evaluation systems that can never capture what you really do in the classroom are just a few of the reasons for this educational exodus. I cannot blame them for leaving the profession. Many teachers are just putting the well-being of their family and themselves first. As a single father, I can totally relate. But at the end of the day, I still teach because it is who I am. It is what I love to do. It's what I choose to do. No formulaic, "cookie-cutter" evaluation system can ever determine how much impact I truly have in the classroom.

My favorite teacher Larry Williams said: "See the world and come back and teach." I would now add: "Teach and you will change the world." Just watch the news every night and you will see this world needs changing. Who is going to be impetus for this change? Will it be the pundits and politicians? I do not think so. Instead, it will be the teachers, all over the world, in the "educational trenches" who will make the difference.

"In the trenches" can have a literal interpretation in this business. Once, during a radio interview after my appearances on *The View*, I was asked: "What do you want parents to know about teachers?" I thought for a moment and came up with this. I said: "We are not perfect. We care and try our best." I then challenged the interviewer to name another profession besides law enforcement in which 99.9% of its members would take a bullet for your kid. This act would be done instinctively, without being armed and without the benefit of body armor. This act is something that the people who came up with our evaluation system have no clue about, but the teachers at Columbine, Virginia Tech, Sandy Hook, and too many others know all too well.

Being a teacher allows me to make a difference. That is the bottom line. Teaching gives me the chance to work with students one on one, empowering them with the knowledge, and critical thinking skills, in an effort to change society. In that way, I make the world a better place.

Being a teacher allows me to use my unique brand of abilities and talents I have acquired through the blend of stand-up comedy and teaching to create a new engagement level with students. Through the Comedy/Teaching Craft and the Stand-Up Teaching Strategies, I can now reach more students who now know that learning and laughter can go hand in hand. In that way the world is a better place.

Being a teacher allows me to pay it forward. My son came to my middle school after a tumultuous time in elementary school. As he entered the 6th grade, he was incredibly shy to the extent of being socially awkward. He suffered from low self-esteem from being bullied in the past. When it came to academics, he was average, but never excelled. By his 8th grade graduation, he made many good friends who accept him unconditionally. He had the confidence that helped him earn his black belt in Tae Kwon Do. He was the Vice President of the National Junior Honors Society. Finally, he was the first student to ever give a keynote address at the 8th grade awards assembly. His last words to me were before he spoke were: "I got this!" I could not have been prouder of him. He had the audience laughing, engaged, with a touch of sentimentality that left them in tears to the point that when he finished he received a standing ovation.

I would like to take credit, but I can't. The real credit, as he pointed out in his speech went to all the wonderful teachers he had over the past 3 years. He specifically noted how they were the ones who were able to give him the confidence to succeed in academics and social development. I can never repay my fellow colleagues for all they have done for my son. I can and will pay it forward by helping my students get the same quality of education that he had. In that way, I make the world better place.

I still teach at a middle school. It is the most crucial time in a student's life. It's that transition phase before all the drama that high school and adulthood have to offer. High schools are large and students can slip through the cracks. Teaching middle school gives me the best chance at engaging them and helping them to turn their lives around while they are still kids.

I have constant reminders of the good I do as teacher in my classroom. I make sure to display photos that students have given me and make a poster collage. My students have been bringing *Sponge Bob* toys for over a decade, which I still display in my classroom. I always make the student sign any memento they give me so I will never forget them. The last day of school, I have all my white boards empty. I leave about a dozen markers and allow students to write one final thought at the end of class. I purposefully do not read any till the last student has left for the day. I am constantly amazed at the thoughtfulness and love the students leave in their messages to me. I make sure to take pictures of all of them. Often the most thoughtful messages come from the quiet or more challenging students who write how much coming to my class has meant to them. It is touches my heart and will often bring me to tears. Tears that remind me that I had made a difference. Tears that make me realize the world is a better place. Tears that remind me why I still teach.

*My School Desk

* Student End of Year Messages to Mr. Rivera

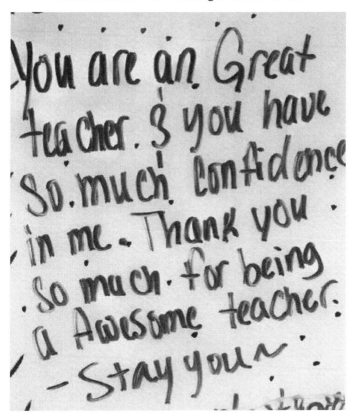

*Student End of Year Messages to Mr. Rivera

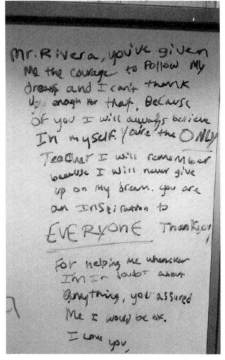

*Student End of Year Messages to Mr. Rivera

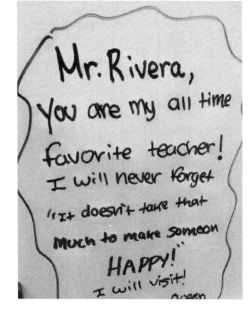

* On EF Educational Tour trip with my son Brendon.

*My wonderful kids Brendon and Caitlin and wonder dog Maurice.

WORKS CITED

Bayard, Caroline. "10 Shocking Things You Probably NEVER Knew About Joan Rivers." *Littlethings.com*. N.p., n.d. Web.

Carter, Judy. *Stand-up Comedy: The Book*. New York, NY: Dell Pub., 1989.

Graham, Byron. "A Field Guide to the Five Worst Types of Hecklers." Westword. N.p., 02 Apr. 2013. Web. 03 May 2015.

Jonas, Peter M. *Laughing and Learning: An Alternative to Shut up and Listen*. Lanham, MD: Rowman & Littlefield Education, 2010. Print.

Lerman, Ali. "K-von Breaks Down Different Types Of Hecklers." *Heard Mentality*. N.p., 13 Oct. 2013. Web. 03 May 2015.

Marzano, Robert J. *The Art and Science of Teaching: A Comprehensive Framework for Effective Instruction*. Alexandria, VA: Association for Supervision and Curriculum Development, 2007. Print.

Marzano, Robert J., Barbara B. Gaddy, and Ceri Dean. *What Works in Classroom Instruction*. Aurora, CO: Mid-continent Research for Education and Learning, 2000. Print.

Marzano, Robert J., Debra Pickering, and Jane E. Pollock. *Classroom Instruction That Works: Research-based Strategies for Increasing Student Achievement*. Alexandria, VA: Association for Supervision and Curriculum Development, 2001. Print.

Marzano, Robert J., Debra Pickering, and Tammy Heflebower. *The Highly Engaged Classroom*. Bloomington, IN: Marzano Research, 2011. Print.

Marzano, Robert J., Jana S. Marzano, and Debra Pickering. *Classroom Management That Works: Research-based Strategies for Every Teacher*.

Alexandria, VA: Association for Supervision and Curriculum Development, 2003. Print.

Marzano, Robert J. *What Works in Schools: Translating Research into Action*. Alexandria, VA: Association for Supervision and Curriculum Development, 2003. Print.

Patrick, Colin. "11 Ways to Handle a Heckler." *Mental Floss*. N.p., 13 Jan. 2013. Web. 03 May 2015.

Wright, Megh. "Eight Types of Hecklers and the Comedians Who Shut Them Up | Splitsider." *Splitsider*. N.p., 14 Mar. 2011. Web. 03 May 2015.

ABOUT THE AUTHORS

America's Most Hilarious Teacher, Mike Rivera, has been a national touring headlining comedian for over 20 years. Mike has been a regular at all the major comedy clubs across the United States, and has appeared on HBO, ShowTime, and on ABC's The View, where he won the "America's Most Hilarious Teacher" competition.

For the past 15 years, Mike has brought humor to his students as a full-time award-winning middle school social studies teacher. In his years of teaching, Mike has been recognized for his innovative comedy/teaching approach.

Mike presently lives in Largo, Florida. He is the proud father of two children and dog, Maurice. He is passionate about travel and exploring the world either by himself, or leading student groups overseas. He loves sports and is an avid fan of the San Francisco Giants, Tampa Bay Lighting, and Tampa Bay Rays

For speaking, appearance, and comedy inquiries, e-mail Mike at Riverams@aol.com.

.

Originally from Lorain, Ohio, **Craig "Sid" Sidorowicz** is an accomplished musician, songwriter, author, and has been a middle school social studies teacher since 2004. Craig is a proud graduate of Bowling Green State University, and is currently pursuing a Master's Degree in Educational Leadership. His interests include collecting, competitive gaming, and martial arts. He presently resides in Largo, Florida with his wife, Kelly, and his two cats, Marigold and Leo.

The Entrepreneur's Publisher